Non-Tech Savvy
SENIORS GUIDE TO
WINDOWS 11

Step-By-Step Illustrated Guide To Mastering Windows 11 Quickly
Stop Asking For Help! Gain The Skills To Manage Your PC On Your Own

3 TECH BONUS

RICK STERLING

TABLE OF CONTENTS

Introduction:

Understanding Windows 11

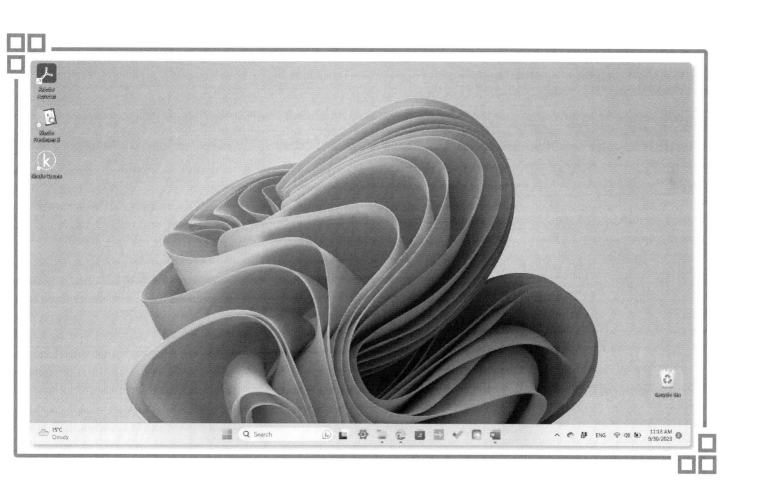

What is Windows 11?

Windows 11 is the latest version of Microsoft's operating system, playing a crucial role in managing software and hardware interactions on computers, laptops, or tablets. This involves efficiently and adequately organizing access to the hard drive, processing unit, memory, and storage space. Starting from Windows 1 in 1985, the Windows versions have evolved through Windows 95, Windows XP, Windows 7, Windows 8, Windows 10, and now to the current Windows 11. Each iteration has brought enhancements in the **user interface and technological advancements** in the background to enrich the computing experience.

Other operating systems like Linux, Ubuntu, Android, ChromeOS, and macOS cater to the diverse needs of users. Some are optimized for tasks such as document creation and email, while others are more suited for software development. Operating systems are also designed for different types of devices; for example, smartphones use Android or iOS, designed for mobile apps, whereas desktops require more comprehensive operating systems to support a wide range of hardware and software.

Windows 11, like its predecessors, offers a Graphical User Interface (GUI), allowing users to interact with their computer through icons and visual cues. This GUI has superseded the older **Character User Interfaces (Cuis)**, where interactions required typed commands.

Why Use Windows?

Windows is a dominant force in the PC and laptop market, except for Apple devices, for several reasons. Its popularity stems from its **user-friendly interface, wide range of compatible applications, backward compatibility, extensive hardware support, plug-and-play functionality, and robust gaming features.**

Microsoft has designed Windows with a consistent and intuitive interface, supporting a vast spectrum of software across different domains. Compatibility with Windows is crucial for software developers looking to capture a significant market share. The OS's backward compatibility ensures that older software versions usually run smoothly on newer Windows versions, protecting users from losing important data or games when upgrading their OS.

Windows' market leadership ensures that hardware and software manufacturers prioritize compatibility, enabling a plug-and-play experience for most peripherals. Moreover, most computer games are optimized for Windows, given its ability to support diverse gaming requirements and enhance performance.

However, Windows has its downsides compared to other operating systems. Its feature-rich environment requires significant resources and compatible hardware, which can become costly. Being a **closed-source OS**, Windows does not allow users to modify its code, unlike open-source alternatives like Linux or Ubuntu. This limitation can be a challenge for those in specialized fields such as software

development or cybersecurity, though it's less of an issue for the average user. Additionally, Windows enforces strict licensing terms that necessitate keeping the system updated, potentially leading to additional costs through subscription plans.

Windows 11 vs. Previous Versions: What's New and What's Gone

The Journey of Windows OS Evolution

This segment aims to shed light on the pivotal advancements and the evolutionary path of the Windows operating system. Grasping these developments allows users to fully appreciate the **enhanced features** and functionalities brought forth by Windows 11, marking a significant leap in the operating system's history.

From the outset with **Windows 1**, Microsoft ventured into the software market, introducing a basic **graphical user interface (GUI)** that enabled user interaction via a mouse-driven cursor. This was a foundational step towards a more intuitive computing experience.

Windows 2 followed, enhancing the visual experience with **16-color display support** and introduced the ability to **minimize and maximize** windows. It also brought keyboard shortcuts into play, along with early versions of Microsoft Word and Excel, marking the beginning of the Office suite.

With **Windows 3**, the distribution of the operating system on **CD-ROM** began. This version introduced various management tools that lessened dependency on command-line interfaces, offering a richer color palette of **256 colors** and embedding **networking capabilities**, a nod towards modern computing requirements.

Windows 95 transitioned closer to what we recognize today, with the **Taskbar** and **Start Menu**. It facilitated internet access through dial-up connections and launched **Internet Explorer**, alongside multimedia enhancements for a richer user experience.

As versions progressed, system demands increased. **Windows 98** required more memory and storage but also supported DVDs and USBs, along with new management features like update and disk cleanup managers.

Windows 2000 aimed at business users, offering **file encryption** and **server capabilities**, while **Windows XP** emerged as a massive hit for its aesthetic appeal and user-friendly design, catering more to home users.

Conversely, **Windows Vista** saw limited success, hampered by higher hardware demands and compatibility issues, while **Windows 7** focused on wireless device needs, enhancing usability through touch, speech, and handwriting recognition.

Windows 8 represented a bold move towards touch interface, a departure that received mixed responses, leading to the more familiar desktop-oriented approach of **Windows 10**. This version reintroduced the Start Menu and introduced **universal apps** and **Cortana**.

Windows 11 Enhancements

Windows 11 introduces a slew of new and significant features absent in its predecessors. Its interface has been described as more **Mac-like**, with a notable change being the **center-aligned Taskbar and Start Menu**. The adoption of a more **pastel color palette** and rounded window corners contributes to a softer visual appeal.

Snap capabilities for window management, the option to create **additional virtual desktops**, and **integration with Android apps** stand out as major functional improvements. **Widgets** have been reimagined to offer dynamic desktop information without impeding performance.

Microsoft Teams integration and simplified access to key settings from the taskbar are notable for enhancing user connectivity and convenience. For gamers, the ability to play **Xbox One games** directly on the PC is a welcome addition.

Security enhancements in Windows 11, including tamper-resistant silicon chips and versatile sign-in options via **Windows Hello**, offer improved protection and convenience.

Removed Features in Windows 11

Some features from previous Windows iterations have been phased out in Windows 11, such as the **movable taskbar** and **Live Tiles** from the Start Menu. The focus on a streamlined and minimalistic design has led to these and other features being discontinued or replaced, reflecting shifts in user preferences and technological advancements.

The reduction in the prominence of **Cortana**, from a staple in Windows 10 to a less visible presence in Windows 11, and the elimination of the taskbar menu right-click options underscore a broader effort to refine and simplify the user interface for enhanced productivity and aesthetics.

In Windows 11, some familiar taskbar functionalities from Windows 10 have been either altered or removed. Notably, the **right-click context menu** on the taskbar has been streamlined to mainly offer taskbar settings, marking a departure from the more comprehensive menu options available in the previous version. Furthermore, the **drag and drop functionality** for files onto taskbar application icons, a feature that facilitated opening files directly in applications, has been disabled.

The **Calendar** feature on the taskbar has seen changes as well. While the calendar itself remains largely unchanged, the convenient list of upcoming events that used to appear beneath the calendar pop-up in Windows 10 is no longer present. Instead, Windows 11 opts for **widgets** for calendar and appointments, offering these details through a different interface rather than directly on the taskbar.

Significant alterations have been made to the **Start menu's appearance**. It now includes a section for **"Pinned apps"**, showcasing application icons, and a **"Recommended apps"** area that highlights some of the most recently or frequently used apps and files. Below these, users can find their user profiles and a power button. This new layout contrasts with the previous version, which featured account and user settings, File Explorer, the Pictures app, power settings, and a comprehensive list of applications.

The earlier Start menu also boasted **live tiles** offering app suggestions, a feature that has been phased out in favor of a more streamlined and simplified design approach in Windows 11.

Determining if your computer is ready for Windows 11 involves evaluating its compatibility against a set of hardware requirements. As with previous versions, Windows 11 demands more advanced resources and hardware for optimal performance. While many computers currently running Windows 10 are expected to support Windows 11 upon its release in early to mid-2022, older models might not meet the necessary criteria. Here are the key hardware prerequisites for running Windows 11 efficiently:

- **Internet Connection**: Essential for downloading Windows 11, though many devices will come with the operating system pre-installed.

- **TPM (Trusted Platform Module)**: Linked to Windows 11's security enhancements, this tamper-proof silicon chip supports encryption services, integral for the security features in Windows 11. Most new devices will include this component.

- **CPU Requirements**: A 64-bit processor with a minimum clock speed of 1GHz is necessary. You can find this information under the "Device Specifications" in the Settings app or listed when purchasing a new device.

- **RAM**: At least 4GB is required, a detail also located in the "Device Specifications" within the Settings app.

- **Storage**: A minimum of 64GB on-device storage is needed to accommodate the operating system's files and potential future updates.

Additionally, Windows 11 operates on **UEFI firmware**, which bridges the OS with the computer's hardware.

For specific CPU compatibility, Windows 11 supports an extensive range of **central processing units**; ensuring your device's processor is on the supported list is crucial for upgrading.

Category	Processors
Intel 8th-14th Gen	8th Gen (Coffee Lake), 9th Gen (Coffee Lake Refresh), 10th Gen (Comet Lake), 10th Gen (Ice Lake), 11th Gen (Rocket Lake), 11th Gen (Tiger Lake), 12th Gen (Alder Lake), 13th Gen (Raptor Lake), 14th Gen (Raptor Lake-S Refresh)
Intel Xeon Series	Xeon Skylake-SP, Xeon Cascade Lake-SP, Xeon Cooper Lake-SP, Xeon Ice Lake-SP
Intel Core X-series	Core X-series

Category	Processors
Intel Xeon® W-series	Xeon® W-series
AMD Ryzen 2000-7000 Series	Ryzen 2000, 3000, 4000, 5000, 6000, 7000 Series
AMD Ryzen Threadripper Series	Ryzen Threadripper 2000, Ryzen Threadripper 3000, Ryzen Threadripper Pro 3000, Ryzen Threadripper Pro 4000
AMD EPYC 2nd-4th Gen	EPYC 2nd Gen, EPYC 3rd Gen, EPYC 4th Gen

This table groups the processors into their respective series, making it easier to understand the wide range of CPUs that support Windows 11.

Upgrading to Windows 11: A Step-by-Step Guide

To upgrade to Windows 11, follow these steps if your device meets the necessary requirements. Microsoft will inform you via a notification if the upgrade is available for your device. However, you can proactively check for the upgrade by following this process:

1) Navigate to **Settings > Update & security > Windows Update**.

2) Click on **Check for Updates**.

3) If your device is eligible, the **Windows 11 feature update** will appear. Select **Download and install**.

The installation process will commence, and it's crucial to follow the on-screen instructions carefully. The upgrade process may take some time, so patience is key.

After installing Windows 11, it's important to **regularly check for updates** to ensure your device continues to run smoothly. Updates can be found in the same section, and Windows will automatically notify you when new updates are available.

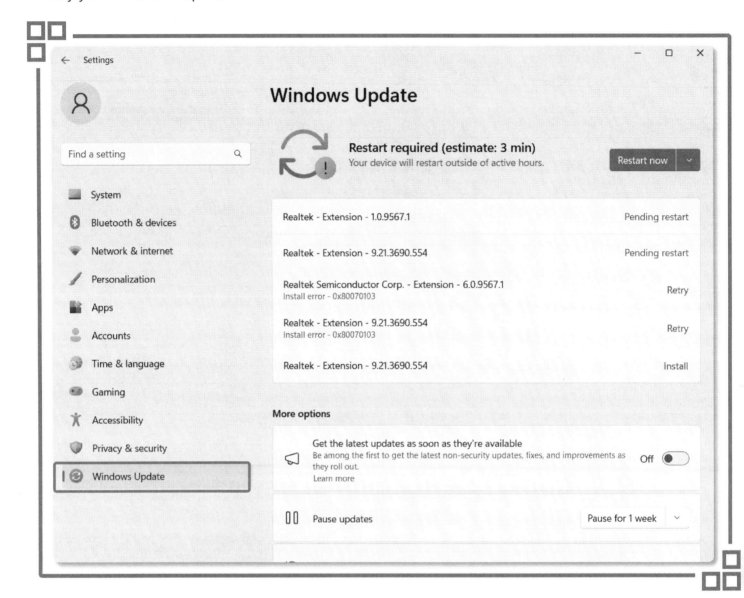

Chapter 1:

Navigating your PC with Windows

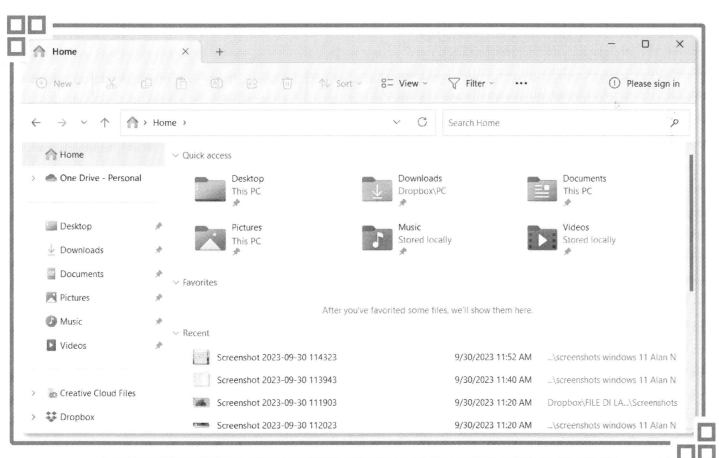

File Explorer

The primary tool for browsing content on a Windows 11 computer is the File Explorer. This comprehensive file management system allows you to locate, organize, and delete all your files, photos, documents, and more.

Overview of File Explorer

Introduced in Windows 95, **File Explorer** has been an integral part of Windows operating systems, continuing through to Windows 11. It serves as a gateway to your computer's drives, libraries, folders, and files, facilitating document searches, file organization, and a multitude of other functions to maintain your computer's content.

With the latest update, File Explorer has undergone a redesign, featuring updated icons for essential folders including Desktop, Documents, Downloads, Music, and more, aligning with the rest of the operating system's refreshed appearance.

Yet, the layout remains user-friendly, and the introduction of vibrant colors brings a fresh, lively look to your File Explorer experience.

Mastering File Explorer in Windows 11

Opening File Explorer:

- Press **Win+E** for a quick launch (the Win key features the Windows 4-panel logo).

- Click the **File Explorer icon** on the taskbar.

- Type **"File Explorer"** into the Start menu search bar.

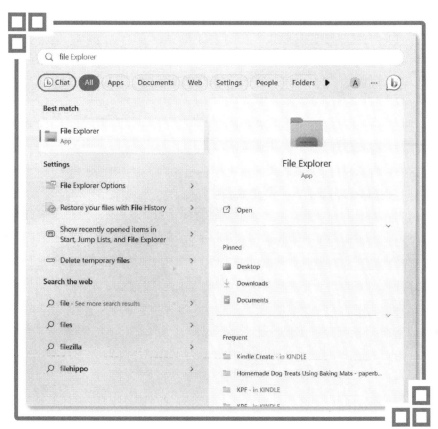

Understanding File Explorer's Interface

In Windows 11, the traditional ribbon bar has been replaced by a streamlined **command bar**, housing essential functions like **Cut, Copy, Paste, Rename, Share, Delete, View,** and **Sort.**

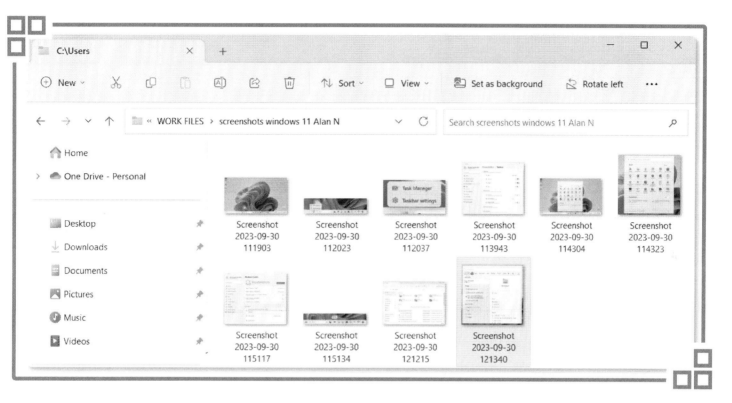

- **View**: Tailor the display of your folders with options for large icons or a detailed list showcasing file sizes and types.

- **Sort**: Organize your content within libraries by criteria such as alphabetical order, modification date, file type, and more. Toggle between ascending and descending order with ease.

- **New**: Easily create a new folder, shortcut, or document. Options for frequently used document formats include text, Microsoft Word documents, Excel spreadsheets, and PowerPoint presentations.

- **See More**: A three-dot icon on the right of the command bar opens additional settings and functions, including:

  - **Undo**: Quickly reverse recent actions, helpful for rectifying accidental deletions or moves.

  - **Pin files to Quick Access**: Highlight files or folders to add them to the Quick Access library on the left side of File Explorer.

- **Context-Sensitive Options**: Depending on the content you're viewing, the command bar adapts to offer relevant tools, like image rotation or setting an image as the desktop background for photos, and networking tools for drive management.

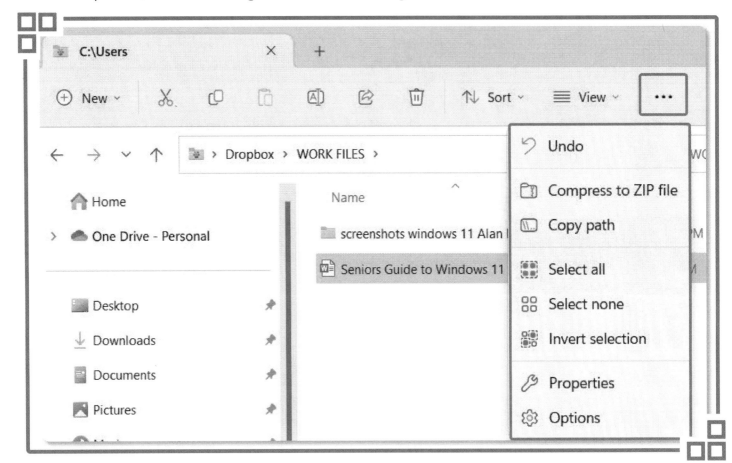

Other functionalities encompass file cleanup, drive optimization or formatting, adding new network locations, mapping network drives, detaching network drives, accessing file or folder properties, and modifying file or folder options.

When you right-click any file or folder within File Explorer, a **context menu** emerges, featuring a fresh look in Windows 11. This menu now places vital options like **Cut, Copy, Rename, Share,** and **Delete** at the forefront, symbolized by intuitive icons for quick identification.

The revamped 'Share' tool introduces a seamless way to distribute content, mirroring the convenience found on mobile devices. Hitting the 'share' icon brings up a dialog showing the number of items you're sharing, with options to dispatch them to frequently contacted individuals via Bluetooth, email through the Mail app, or through an array of other applications.

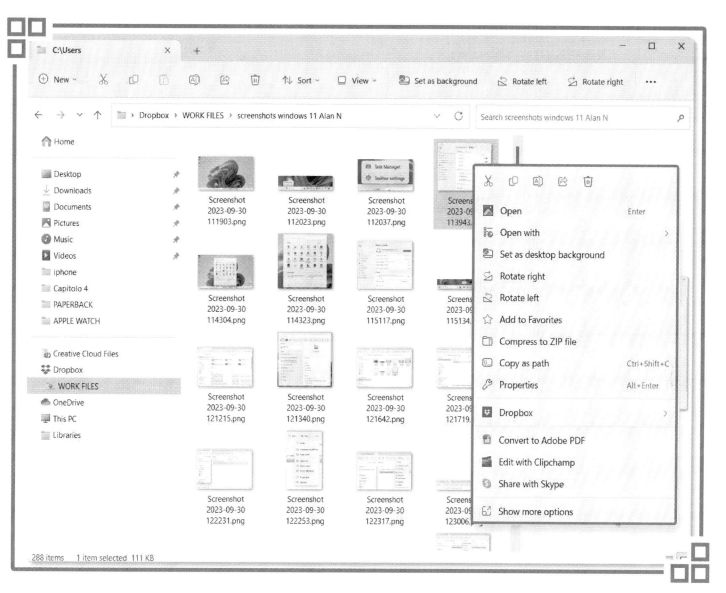

Copy & Paste Files and Folders

In Windows 11, the process of copying and pasting files has been made more straightforward than ever. The Command bar now includes dedicated copy and paste buttons, simplifying the task of moving your data. **To copy files**, simply select and highlight the desired files and click the Copy button.

This action copies the selected items to the 'clipboard'. Alternatively, you can select the files, press **Ctrl+C** on your keyboard, navigate to the target location, and then click the Paste button or press **Ctrl+V.** This method transfers the items to a new location without altering the originals, allowing you to access them in their initial locations.

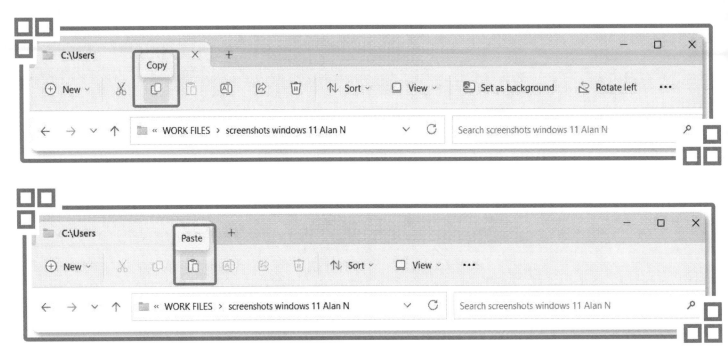

Utilizing the Cut Function for Files and Folders

The **cut tool** offers a way to move files or folders from one location to another by temporarily storing them on the clipboard. It operates similarly to the copy function but with a key difference. After selecting the desired files or folders and clicking the **Cut button** or pressing **Ctrl+X**, you can move them to a new location.

Pasting the cut items removes them from their original location, effectively preventing the accumulation of unnecessary duplicates in your libraries. Cutting is especially useful when you need to organize or declutter your files without leaving behind redundant copies.

Accessing File and Folder Properties in Windows 11

To delve into the specifics of a file or folder, such as its name, type (e.g., Word document, Excel spreadsheet, JPEG image), content details, size, parent folder location, available space in the parent folder, and the creation date and time, you can easily access its properties in Windows 11.

To view the properties:

1) Navigate to the desired file or folder in File Explorer.

2) Click on the **"show more"** button represented by the three dots on the command bar. This action reveals a menu with various options, with **'Properties'** located at the bottom.

3) Alternatively, right-click on the file or folder, scroll to the bottom of the context menu, and select **'Properties'**.

This process provides a comprehensive overview of important details about your files or folders, offering insights into their composition and status on your disk drive.

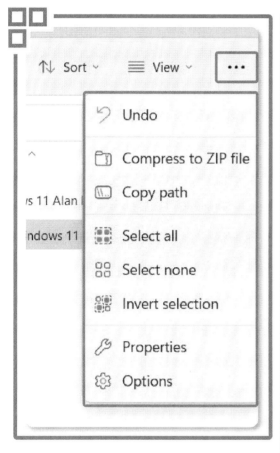

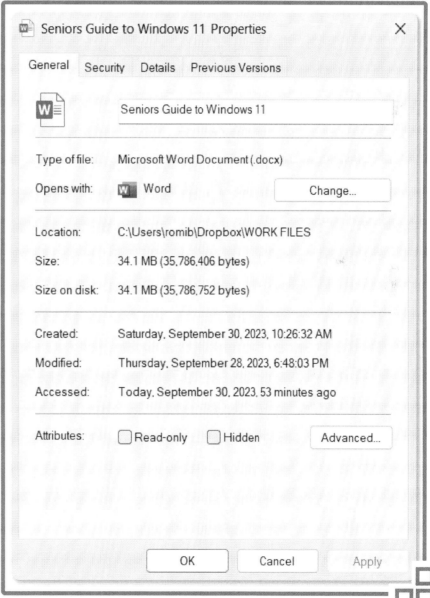

Leveraging the View Button in File Explorer

In Windows 11, the **View button** on the Command bar revolutionizes how you display your files and folders, offering a versatile range of viewing options. Whether you prefer your icons extra large for better visibility or tiny for maximum screen real estate, the View button caters to all preferences. Besides icon size adjustments (extra large, large, medium, or small), you have the option to display items as a list, with details, as tiles, or as content.

Compact View is a notable feature for reducing the space between files and folders. This is particularly useful on touch-enabled devices, as it enlarges the spacing making it easier to select items with a finger. However, for those using a mouse or preferring a denser layout, compact view can be toggled on or off as needed.

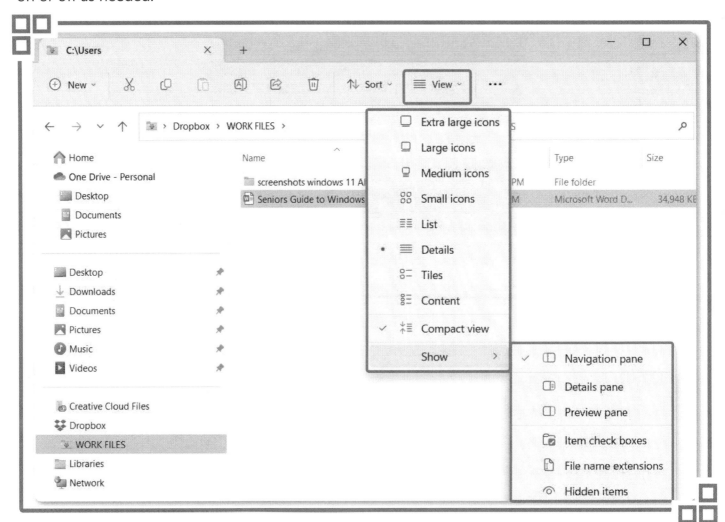

The View button also allows you to customize the information displayed in File Explorer:

- **Navigation Pane**: Situated on the left side of the window, this pane offers quick access to key libraries on your computer, including the Quick Access, OneDrive, This PC, and Network locations. The Quick Access section itself contains shortcuts to frequently used folders like Desktop,

Downloads, Documents, Pictures, Music, and Videos. You have the flexibility to show or hide the Navigation Pane as per your preference.

- **Details Pane and Preview Pane**: Enhance your file management by choosing to display additional information about a selected item or a preview of the item's content.

- **Item Check Boxes, File Name Extensions, and Hidden Items**: Customize your view further by deciding whether to show check boxes for easy selection, extensions for all file types, or hidden files and folders within File Explorer.

With these customizable view options, Windows 11's File Explorer allows for a tailored browsing experience, accommodating both touch and traditional mouse and keyboard inputs efficiently.

The **Details and Preview Panes** augment the File Explorer's functionality by providing essential information or visual previews of the selected items. Positioned on the right side of the File Explorer window, these panes enrich your browsing experience:

- **Details Pane**: Offers a concise summary of the selected file or folder, including its name, type, last updated date, size, and the date it was created.

- **Preview Pane**: Gives you a sneak peek of the content within a file, allowing you to scroll through different pages of a document without opening it fully.

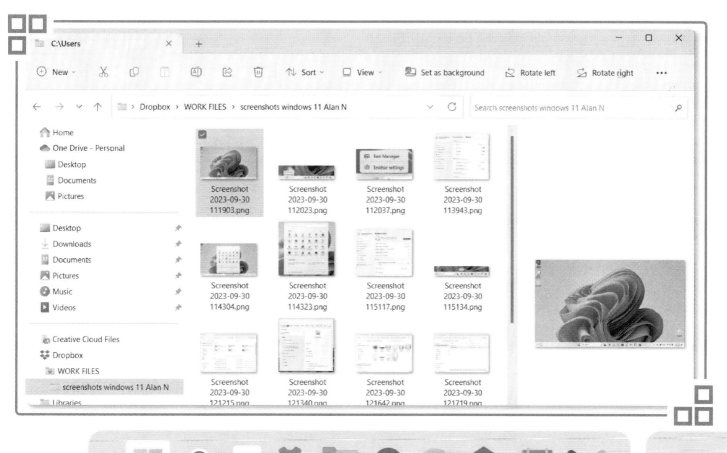

Item Check Boxes, a novel addition in Windows 11 tailored for touch-screen users, simplifies the selection process for multiple files or folders. Activating this feature displays small checkboxes over items in File Explorer, facilitating bulk actions like moving, copying, or deleting with ease. This functionality mirrors the action of holding down the **Ctrl** key while clicking multiple items with a mouse.

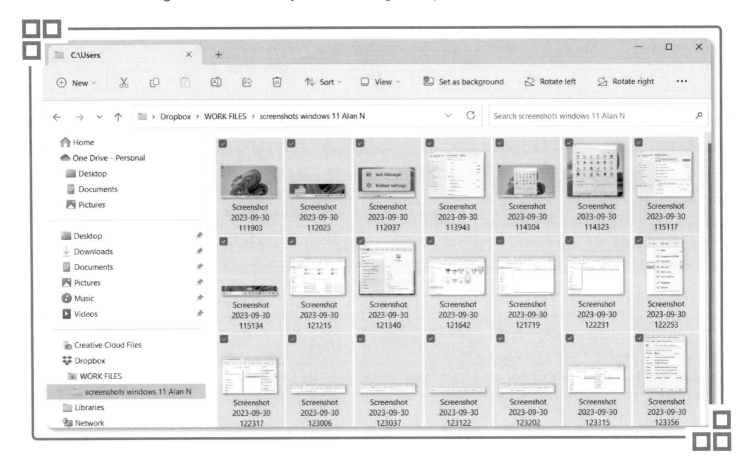

File Extensions visibility is now a toggleable option within File Explorer. These extensions, typically three or four characters long at the end of a file name, signify the file's format, guiding Windows on how to handle the file. Examples include .JPEG, .PNG, .DOCX, .XLS, .PPT, and .ZIP. Showing or hiding these extensions can help users identify file types at a glance or streamline the visual clutter, respectively.

Hidden Items: The View Menu in Windows 11 also includes the ability to reveal or conceal hidden files and folders. Many of these are tucked away by default, often housing critical system data not meant for routine modification. The **Hidden Items** toggle provides control over the visibility of these files, allowing users to access them when necessary.

Utilizing the Sort Button

The **Sort button** in File Explorer maintains its traditional role, enabling users to organize files and folders based on various criteria such as name, type, size, creation date, modification date, authors, tags, or title.

This functionality extends the flexibility to display sorted content in either ascending or descending order, offering diverse perspectives like sorting files by size from largest to smallest or arranging names alphabetically from A to Z.

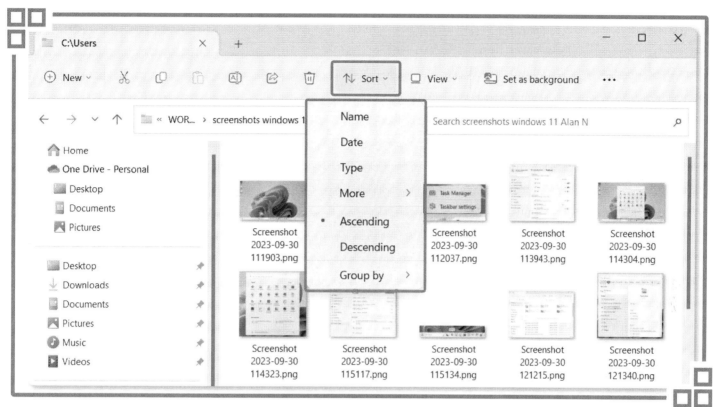

Creating New Folders in File Explorer

Creating a new folder in Windows 11's File Explorer is straightforward. Simply click on the **'New'** option located on the Command Bar's left side to reveal a menu offering choices to create a new folder, shortcut, or document types like Microsoft Word documents, Excel spreadsheets, and PowerPoint presentations. Initiating any of these options automatically opens the relevant program for immediate work on the new item.

Transferring Files Across Folders

To move files within File Explorer, start by selecting the desired files, either by holding **Ctrl** while clicking or using the item checkboxes. Once selected, you have two primary methods to move them:

- **Drag and Drop**: Ideal for mouse users, this method involves clicking, holding, and dragging the selected files to their new location.

- **Copy and Paste**: Achievable with **Ctrl+C** and **Ctrl+V** shortcuts or via the Command Bar's copy and paste icons. Alternatively, cutting and pasting with **Ctrl+X** and **Ctrl+V** moves the files without leaving duplicates.

Deleting Unwanted Files or Folders

File Explorer allows for file or folder deletion by selecting them and clicking the **'Delete'** button on the Command Bar. A right-click also offers a delete option via the context menu. For permanent deletion bypassing the Recycle Bin, use **Shift + Delete**. Remember, this action makes recovery from the Recycle Bin impossible.

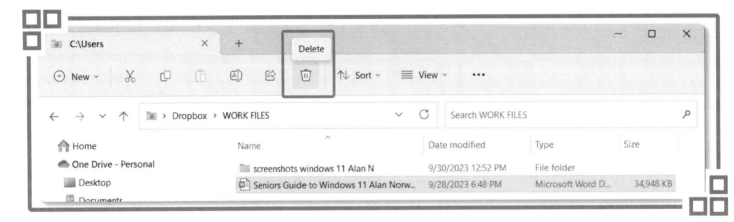

Locating Files and Folders

Searching for files or folders is a breeze in File Explorer, thanks to the Search bar. Simply type in the desired file or folder name, and the search results will be displayed promptly.

Reversing Actions

Mistaken actions, like accidental deletions or movements, can be quickly undone with **Ctrl+Z** for undoing and **Ctrl+Y** for redoing.

Restoring Deleted Files from the Recycle Bin

Windows 11 continues to store deleted items temporarily in the Recycle Bin. Access it directly from its desktop icon or via File Explorer's address bar by typing "Recycle Bin". Within the Bin, select the items you wish to restore and click the restore option in the Command Bar to return them to their original location.

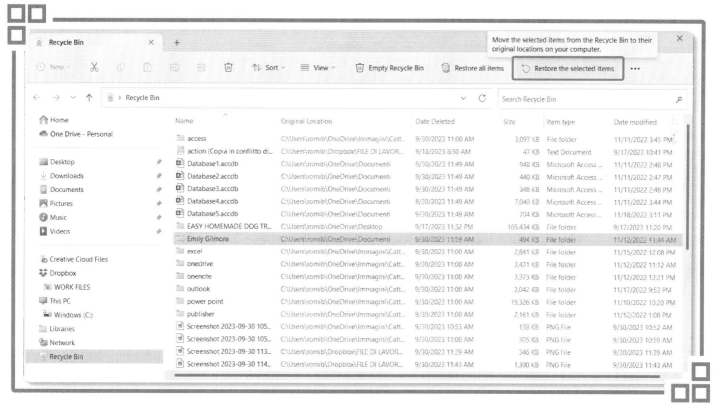

If the Recycle Bin icon is missing from your desktop, adjusting your settings can easily bring it back:

1) Open **Settings > Personalization > Themes**.

2) Scroll to find **"Desktop icon settings"**.

3) Ensure the **Recycle Bin checkbox** is ticked to display the icon on your desktop.

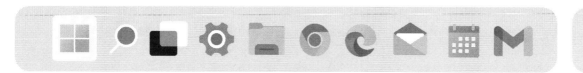

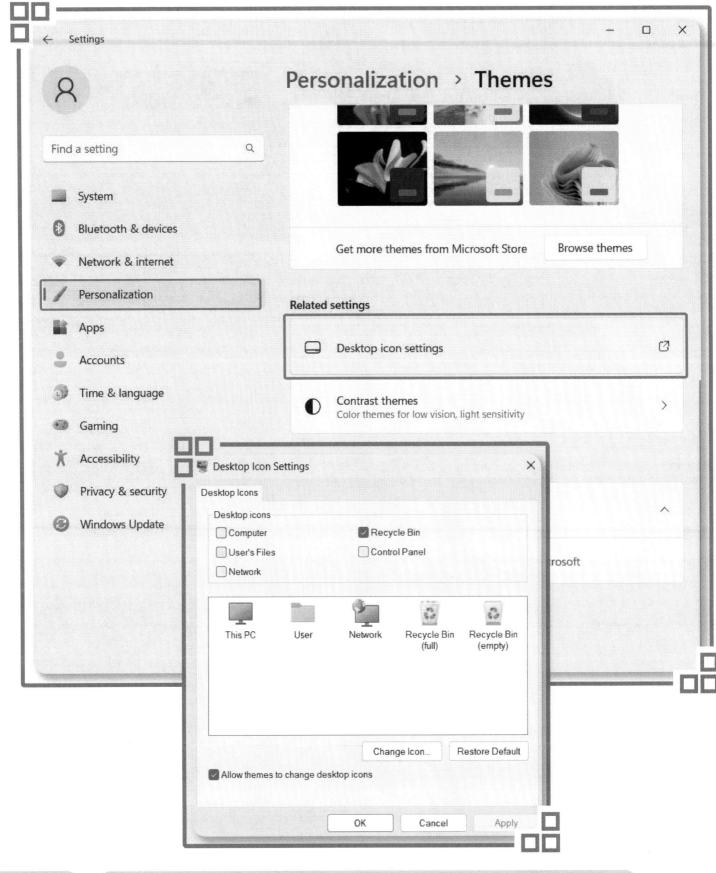

Chapter 2:

Mastering Settings Management in Windows 11

Windows 11 allows for a broad array of settings adjustments, enabling you to tailor your computing experience, whether for work or leisure. This chapter will guide you through navigating and customizing some of the key settings to enhance your user experience.

Accessing the Settings App

The Settings App in Windows 11 serves as the central hub for all your configuration needs, from customization and installation to connectivity and account settings. Here are several ways to access the Settings App:

- Click the **Start Menu** and locate the cogwheel symbol for Settings.

- Drag and drop the Settings icon to the taskbar for easy access, or right-click the app icon and select **"Pin to taskbar."**

- Open the Start Menu and type **'settings'** to search directly for the Settings app icon.

- Choose **"All apps"** from the Start Menu and find the Settings App, which is listed alphabetically among other applications.

- Utilize the keyboard shortcut **Windows Key + I** to open Settings instantly.

- Click the **Quick Settings** button on the right side of the taskbar to reveal a flyout menu with an icon linking directly to the Settings App in the lower-right corner.

Once inside, the Settings App presents various categories within a navigation pane on the left side of the window, defaulting to the System settings upon opening. Within the System section, you will find settings for:

- **Display**
- **Sound**
- **Notifications**
- **Focus Assistant**
- **Power and Battery**
- **Storage**
- **Nearby Sharing**
- **Multitasking**
- **Activation**
- **Troubleshoot**
- **Recovery**
- **Projecting to This PC**
- **Remote Desktop**
- **Clipboard**
- **About**

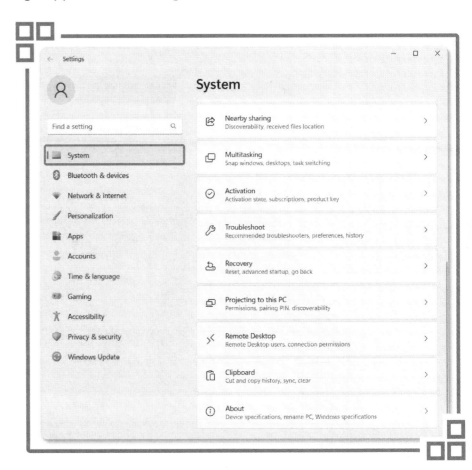

These settings provide a broad spectrum of customization opportunities, ranging from configuring your screen display and sound to managing power settings and accessing system information. This ensures that your experience with Windows 11 can be both personalized and optimized for efficiency.

Understanding Microsoft and Local Accounts

Since Windows 10's debut, Microsoft has promoted the use of Microsoft accounts for logging into PCs and laptops. A **Microsoft account** is free and integrates with online services like OneDrive, Xbox Live, Skype, and Microsoft 365, requiring an internet connection for full functionality.

Alternatively, a **local account** offers a more traditional sign-in method without internet services, using just a username and password stored locally.

Benefits of a Microsoft Account

- Access to a wide range of online services.
- Automatic full-disk encryption of the system drive.
- Storage and protection of data on OneDrive.
- Subscription and activation data linked to the account for easy Windows reinstallation.
- Synchronization of preferences across devices.
- Easy password recovery via email, unlike the more challenging local account password retrieval.

How to Register for a Microsoft Account

1) Visit the Microsoft website at **signup.live.com** or follow prompts during Windows 11 installation.
2) Opt to use an existing email or create a new one by choosing **"Get a new email address."**
3) Fill out the form with your details and select a username.
4) Create a strong password to complete the registration.
5) Sign in with this account after installing Windows 11.

Creating a New Local Account

Windows 11 requires a Microsoft account for installation but allows switching to a local account afterward:

1) Go to **Settings App > Account > Your information**.
2) Click **"Sign in with a local account instead."**
3) Follow prompts to sign out of the Microsoft account and create a local account with a username and recommended password.
4) Sign out and log back in with the new local account.

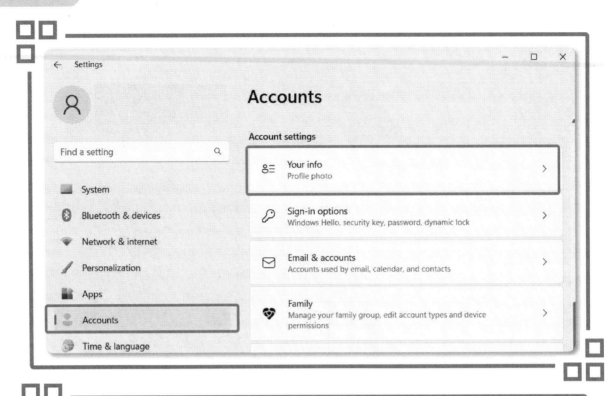

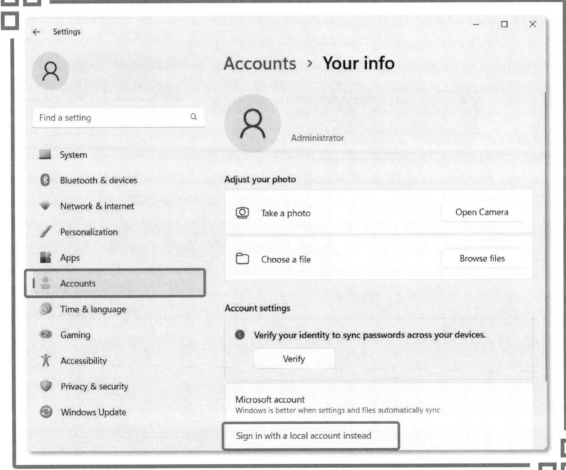

Options for Sign-In

Sign-In Options with Windows Hello

Windows 11 offers various secure sign-in methods through Windows Hello, including a password, PIN, facial recognition, or fingerprint scanning:

1) Navigate to **Start > Settings App > Accounts > Sign-in options > Set up > Get started**.
2) Choose your preferred sign-in method and follow on-screen instructions to configure.

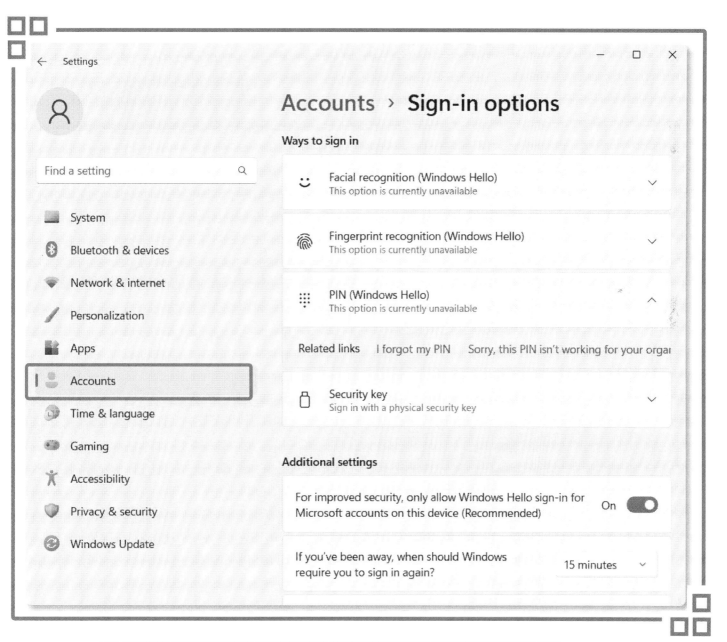

Changing Your Windows Hello PIN

To change your PIN:

1) Go to **Start > Settings > Accounts > Sign-in settings**.
2) Click **PIN > Change PIN** and follow prompts, starting with entering your current PIN.

Changing Your Microsoft Account Password

Microsoft encourages moving away from passwords in favor of options like PIN due to security:

1) For password changes, go to **Settings > Accounts > Sign-in options > Password > Change your password**.
2) Follow prompts, including entering your current and a new password with a hint.

If using Windows Hello sign-in, password changes for your Microsoft account need to be done through account.microsoft.com, following security procedures including a one-time code verification.

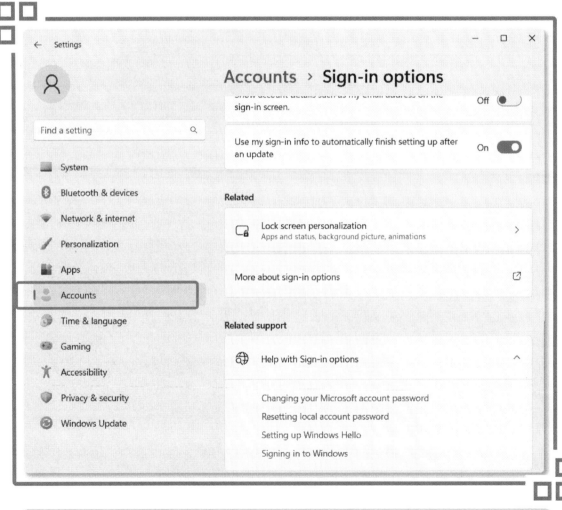

Navigating Personalization Settings

Accessing personalization options on your Windows 11 device is straightforward. Simply **right-click on the desktop** and select **'Personalization'** from the context menu to explore customization settings. Additionally, these settings are available through the **Settings app** under the personalization section.

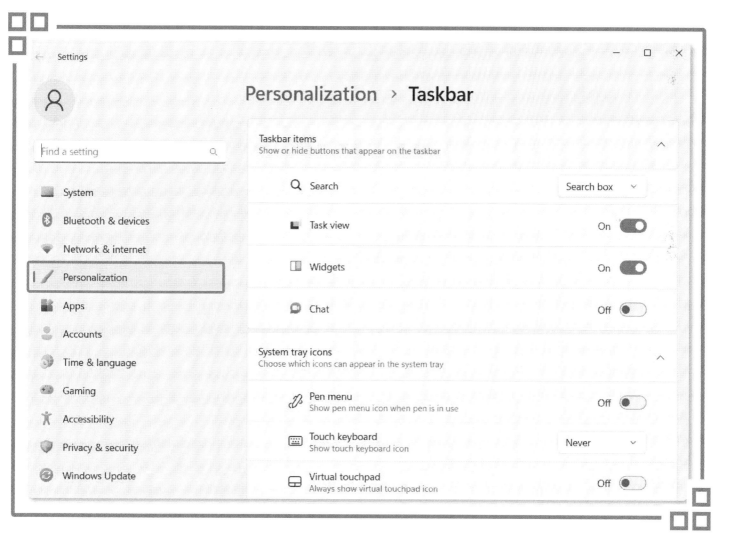

Customizing the Taskbar

Although the Taskbar in Windows 11 is by default located at the bottom of the screen, you have the flexibility to tweak various aspects according to your preferences.

Aligning Taskbar Items to the Left

For those who favor the traditional left-aligned layout of the Taskbar, adjustments can be made easily:

1) Navigate to **Settings App > Personalization > Taskbar > Taskbar behaviors**.
2) Here, you'll find the option to align the icons to the left or center of the screen, allowing you to choose your preferred layout.

Auto-Hiding the Taskbar

To maximize screen real estate, you can set the taskbar to auto-hide:

1) Within the same **Taskbar behaviors** settings, activate the **auto-hide feature**.
2) This makes the Taskbar disappear from view when not in use, reappearing when the mouse is moved to the bottom of the screen.

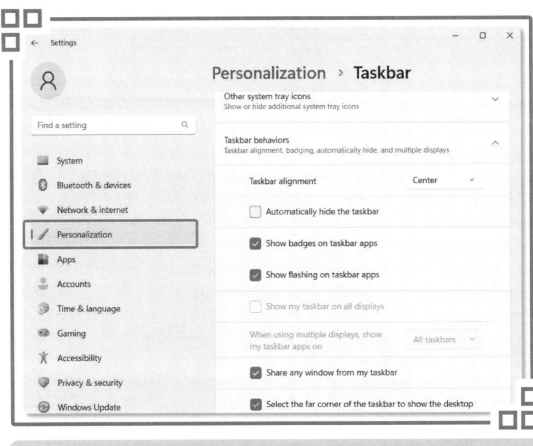

Modifying the Taskbar's Appearance

Changing the color or applying a translucent effect to your taskbar enhances the overall look of your desktop. This can be accomplished through the **Settings > Personalization > Colors** section. Here's how:

1) Select **'Custom'** from the **"Choose your mode"** dropdown.
2) Pick **'Dark'** for the **"Choose your default Windows mode."**
3) Scroll to find and check the **"Show accent color on Start and Taskbar"** option.
4) Set the accent color to **'Manual'** and choose your preferred color from the palette provided.

Pinning Apps for Quick Access

Ensuring your most-used apps are easily accessible can streamline your workflow. Pinning apps to the taskbar allows for this convenience:

To pin apps from the Start menu, navigate to **"All apps"**, right-click on the desired app, and select **"Pin to taskbar."** If the option isn't directly visible, click **'More'** and then choose **"Pin to Taskbar."**

Desktop applications can be pinned by right-clicking on their icons and selecting **"Pin to Taskbar."**

For apps currently running, their icons will be visible on the taskbar with a line underneath. Right-click these icons and select **"Pin to Taskbar"** to keep them there permanently.

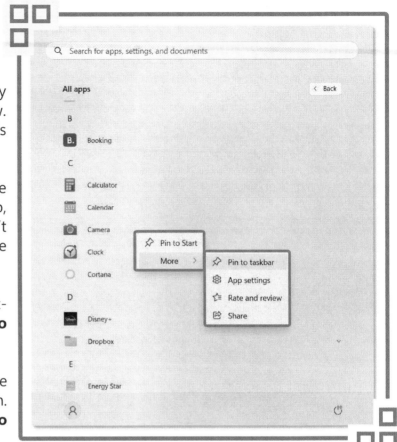

Removing an App from the Taskbar

To unpin an app from the taskbar, simply right-click on its icon and choose **"Unpin from taskbar."** Note that certain icons, such as the Start Menu, Search, Task View, Widgets, and Chat, are fixed and cannot be removed. However, you can hide the latter four:

Go to **Settings > Personalization > Taskbar** and locate the section for taskbar items.

Use the sliders to hide these app icons from your taskbar, keeping your workspace tidy and tailored to your needs.

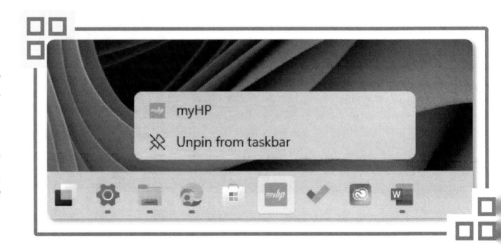

Managing Notifications and the Taskbar Corner in Windows 11

Hiding App Badges on the Taskbar

Windows 11 allows apps like Chat to display badges, such as a counter for unread messages. If preferred, you can disable these notifications:

- Navigate to **Settings > Personalization > Taskbar > Taskbar behaviors** to turn off badge notifications for specific apps.

Customizing the Taskbar Corner

The taskbar corner, positioned on the right side of your taskbar, houses quick access icons for functions including the keyboard, battery, volume, and language settings. This feature aims to reduce desktop clutter while maintaining accessibility to various controls.

Clicking the taskbar overflow corner reveals the **Quick Settings flyout menu**, which shows all available icons and their current status. Default settings include:

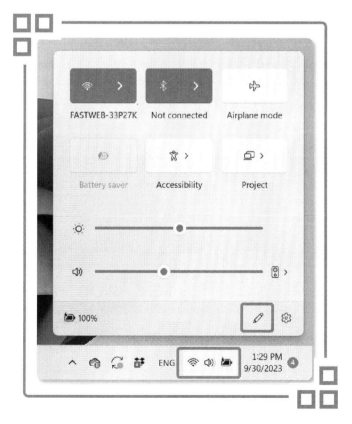
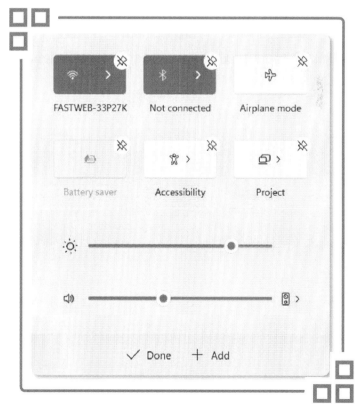

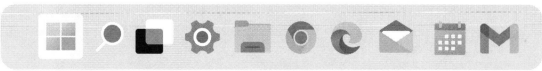

- **Internet connectivity**
- **Bluetooth**
- **Flight mode**
- **Battery saving**
- **Focus assistant**
- **Accessibility**
- **Casting**
- **Volume**
- **Brightness adjustments**

At the bottom of the flyout menu, icons for editing (**pencil icon**) and accessing the full settings app (**cogwheel icon**) are available. The pencil icon allows you to pin or unpin options from this menu, and the cogwheel directs you to the comprehensive settings application.

Configuring System Tray Icons

Certain icons, such as the Pen menu, Touch keyboard, and Visual touchpad, can be turned on or off depending on your device's input capabilities. To manage these icons:

- Go to **Settings > Personalization > Taskbar**, and toggle these options according to your preferences.

The **taskbar corner overflow**, accessible via a small up arrow in the taskbar corner, lets you manage which app icons appear in this overflow tray.

Adjustments can be made within the taskbar settings under **Taskbar corner overflow** to customize which programs are displayed, enhancing your taskbar's functionality and appearance.

Customizing the Start Menu in Windows 11

Adding or Removing Pinned Apps

- To **add** an app to the Start menu, navigate to "All apps" within the Start menu, locate the desired app, right-click on it, and select "Pin to Start."

- To **remove** an app from the Start menu, right-click on its icon and choose "Unpin from Start."

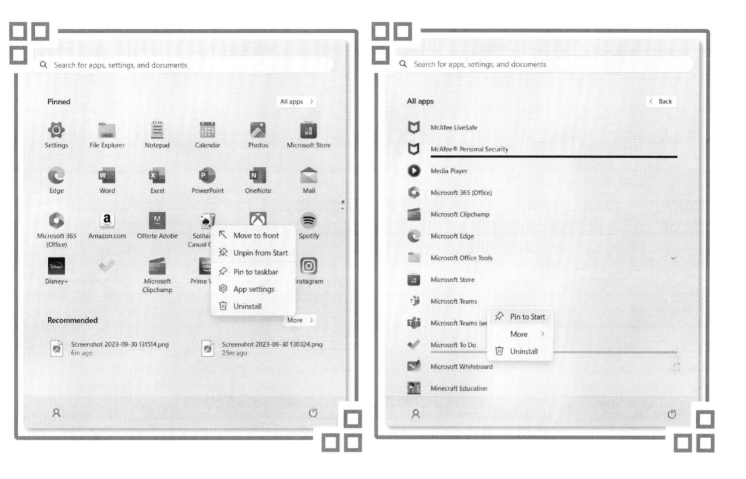

Customizing Folders Next to the Power Button

You can personalize which folders appear next to the Start menu's power button:

1) Go to **Settings > Personalization > Start > Folders**.
2) Here, you can select the folders you frequently use to display them next to the power button for easy access.

Changing the Start Menu Color

Adjusting your taskbar's color also affects the Start menu. To customize:

1) Visit **Settings > Personalization > Colors**.

2) Choose 'Custom' from the **"Choose your mode"** dropdown and select **'Dark'** for the **"Choose your default Windows mode."**

3) Scroll down to enable **"Show accent color on Start and Taskbar."**

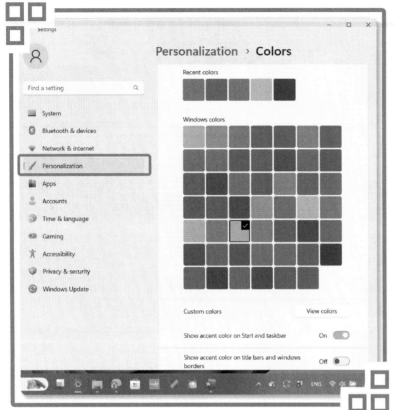
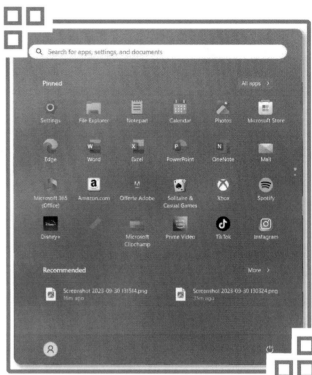

Optimizing Performance by Disabling Transparency Effects

If your PC experiences lag while opening or closing programs, consider disabling transparency effects to alleviate GPU strain and enhance performance:

- This option can be found under **Settings > Personalization > Colors**, where you can toggle transparency effects off.

Hiding Recently Installed and Most Used Apps

Windows 11 typically showcases recently installed and frequently used apps in the Start menu. To hide these:

1) Access **Settings > Personalization > Start**.
2) Adjust your preferences to hide these app categories.

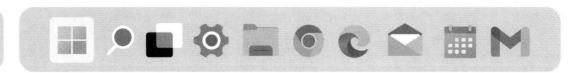

Pin Collections

While direct pinning of files or folders to the Start menu is not available, you can pin key libraries for quick access:

- Open **Settings** > **Personalization** > **Start** > **Folders** and activate the libraries you wish to pin to the Start menu.

Customizing Your Lock Screen and Desktop Background in Windows 11

Customizing the Lock Screen

The Lock Screen, showing the time and date over your chosen background, can be personalized in a few steps:

1) Go to **Settings** > **Personalization** > **Lock screen**.

2) Choose your preferred lock screen background: a single image, a slideshow of images, or Windows Spotlight for daily Bing images.

These adjustments offer a more tailored and efficient user experience, allowing Windows 11 to fit your personal style and workflow preferences.

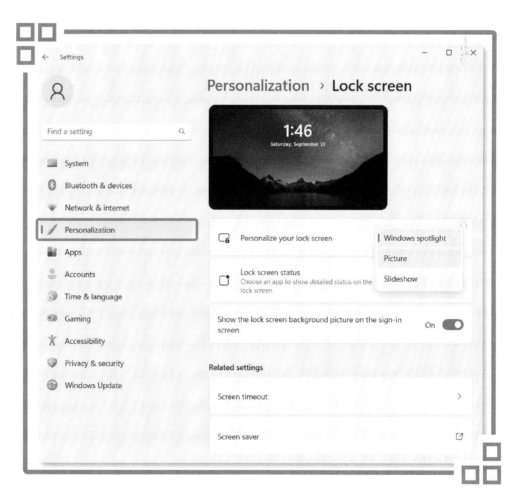

Windows 11 allows you to display information from specific applications on your Lock Screen, offering both utility and personalization.

Options include:

- **3D Viewer**: Ideal for mobile devices with an accelerometer, creating a 3D Parallax effect.

- **Weather**: Stay updated with the current weather conditions.

- **Amazon**: Quick access to your Amazon shopping.

- **Xbox Console Companion**: Keep in touch with your gaming achievements and friends.

- **Mail**: Get a glance at your latest emails.

- **Calendar**: View your upcoming appointments.

You can select only one application to show its information on the Lock Screen.

Setting Up a Slideshow Background

To have a rotating selection of images as your Desktop background:

- Create an album in the settings app, with options to customize the frequency of image change and whether the sequence should be shuffled.

Opting for a Solid Color Background:

For a simpler aesthetic, select **"Solid color"** instead of 'Slideshow' or 'Picture'.

Personalizing Backgrounds for Different Desktops:

Windows 11 enables setting distinct backgrounds for each of your virtual desktops, allowing for a customized experience based on use case, such as:

A professional background for work-related desktops and a personal photo for leisure desktops. Access this feature by selecting "Personalize your background," then right-click on the chosen image to see options like **"Set for all desktops"** or **"Set for desktop."** Choose "Set for desktop" to apply your selection to a specific desktop.

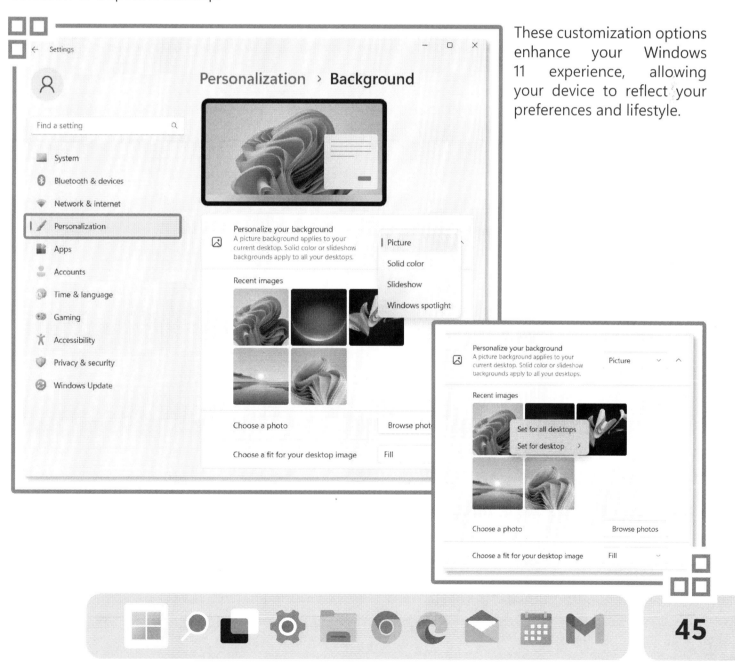

These customization options enhance your Windows 11 experience, allowing your device to reflect your preferences and lifestyle.

Tailoring Windows 11 to Your Style: Customization Guide

Switching Between Dark Mode and Light Mode

Windows 11 lets you switch between **Dark Mode** and **Light Mode**, impacting the taskbar, Start menu, desktop wallpaper, windows, and sound schemes. Dark Mode features light text on dark backgrounds with subdued sounds, while Light Mode offers black text on light backgrounds with vibrant wallpapers and alert sounds. To toggle between these modes, head to **Settings > Personalization > Colors**.

Exploring Themes

Themes bundle together wallpapers, color schemes, sounds, and other customizations.

Windows 11 includes themes like Windows Dark, Windows Light, Glow, Captured Motion, Sunrise, and Flow, with more available for download.

Customize your theme via **Settings > Personalization > Themes**, choosing backgrounds, color schemes, sounds, and cursor styles.

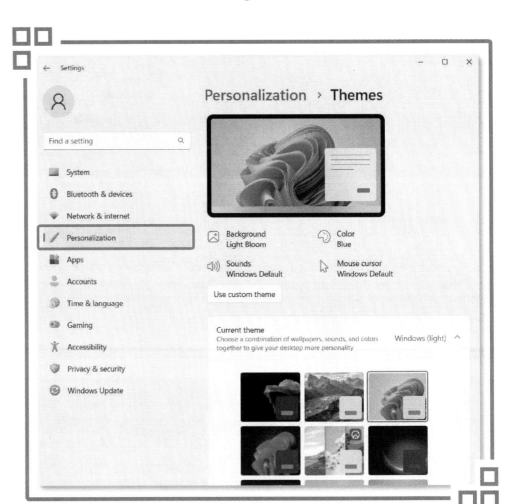

Adjusting Scaling for Clarity

Windows 11 aims to automatically resize screen elements for visibility, but you might need larger text, icons, and other elements. High-resolution screens or multi-monitor setups may require adjustments. Navigate to **Settings > Display > Scale and layout** to find scaling and resolution options. Typically, 100% scale is recommended, but you can adjust according to your screen size and preference.

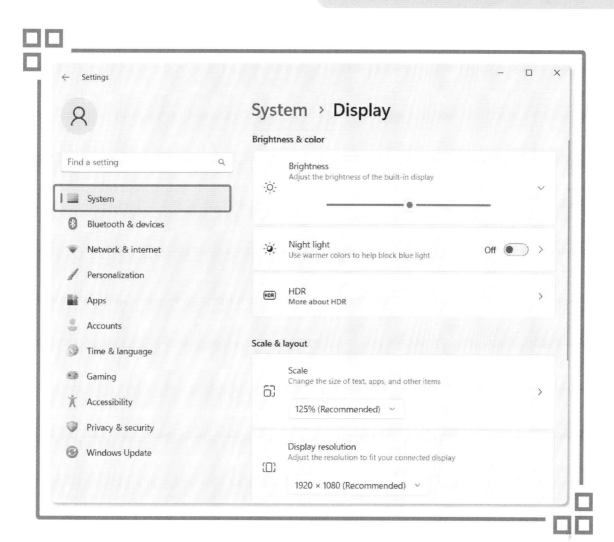

Connecting Bluetooth Devices

For Bluetooth-enabled devices, ensure Bluetooth is active under **Settings > Bluetooth & devices**.

Click **Add device** to start searching for nearby Bluetooth devices. Make sure the device you're pairing is on and in pairing mode.

Devices previously paired will automatically connect if Bluetooth is enabled, which can also be toggled quickly in the **Quick settings** menu on the taskbar corner.

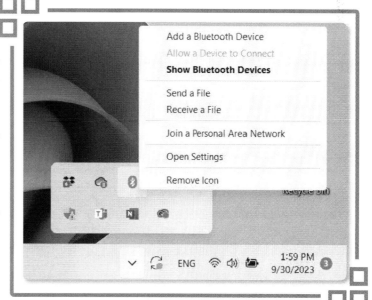

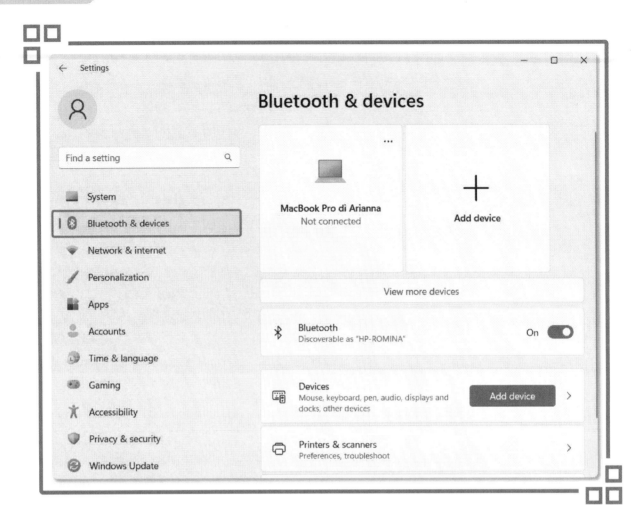

Setting Up Scanners or Printers

Windows 11 facilitates the discovery and driver installation for network or wireless printers and scanners.

To add a new device, ensure it's on and connected, then go to **Settings > Bluetooth & Devices > Printers & Scanners** and hit **Refresh**. If your device doesn't appear, older models may require selecting "The printer that I want isn't listed" for manual addition.

For wireless printers, ensure they're on the same network as your computer.

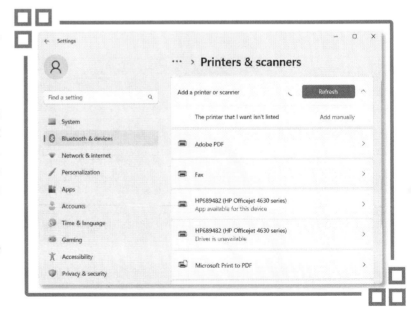

These customization and setup options enhance the personal and professional use of Windows 11, making your computing experience both unique and efficient.

Connecting Your Android Phone to Your Windows 11 PC

Windows 11 enhances connectivity with your Android device through the "Your Phone" app, streamlining the synchronization of photos, videos, messages, calls, notifications, and more.

1) Open the "Your Phone" app by navigating to **Settings > Bluetooth & Devices > Your Phone > Open Your Phone**.

2) Ensure your Android phone is nearby and click **"Get Started."** You might need to sign in to your Microsoft account if prompted.

3) Install the **"Your Phone Companion - Link to Windows"** app on your Android phone, available through the Google Play Store or at **www.aka.ms/yourpc**.

4) After installation, on your PC, select **"I have the Your Phone Companion - Link to Windows App ready"** and then **"Pair with QR code"**. A QR code will be displayed on your PC screen.

5) Open the **"Your Phone Companion"** app on your Android phone, select **"Link your phone and PC,"** then **"Continue,"** and scan the QR code shown on your PC.

6) Follow the instructions to complete the setup and click **'Done.'** Your Android phone is now connected to your PC.

Now, you can access your phone's messages, notifications, media, and calls directly from the "Your Phone" app on your Windows 11 PC.

Projecting Your Computer Screen Wirelessly

Wireless displays allow you to project your computer screen onto a larger monitor or smart TV without cables.

1) To enable this feature, go to **Settings > Apps > Optional features > Add an optional feature > View features**. Type "wireless display" in the search bar, select it, and click **Next** followed by **Install**.

2) Once installed, you may find **"Wireless display"** listed under Optional features in the Apps settings. A system restart might be required to apply the changes.

3) For configuring wireless projection, navigate to **Settings > System > Projecting to this PC**. Change the setting from "Always Off" to **"Available everywhere on secure networks"** or **"Available everywhere"**.

4) Then, choose **"Launch the Connect app to project to this PC"** to allow devices on the same network to connect to your Windows 11 PC.

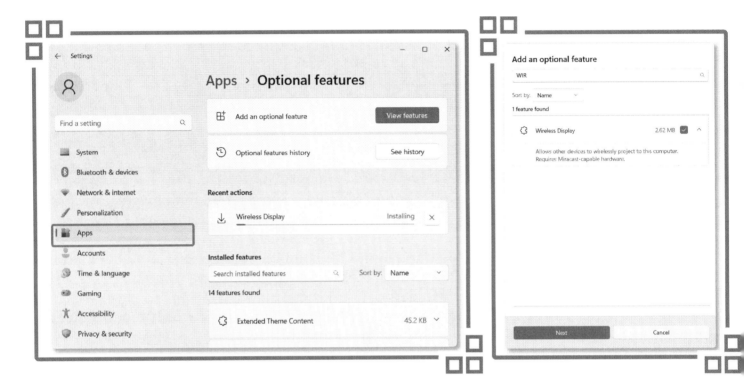

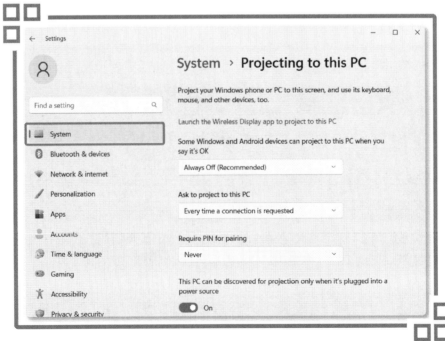

Chapter 3:

Enhancing Accessibility for Senior Users in Windows 11

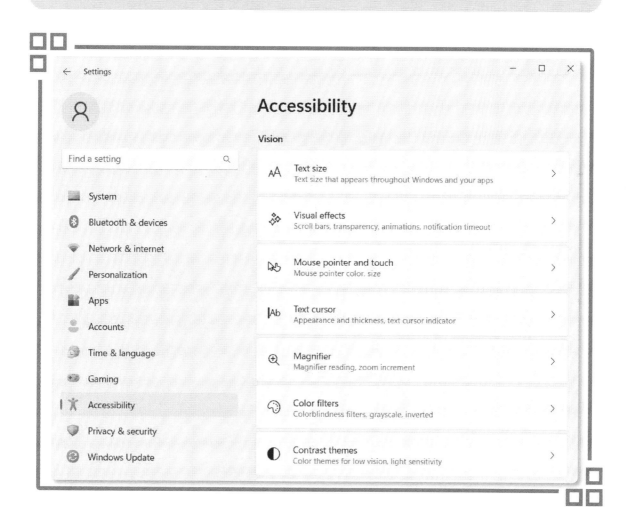

Implementing Contrast Themes

To aid users with visual impairments, Windows 11 introduces **contrast themes** which provide a stark contrast between UI elements, enhancing readability.

Default themes include Aquatic, Desert, Dusk, and Night Sky. Access these by navigating to **Settings > Accessibility > Contrast themes**.

A quick switch between high contrast and regular themes is achievable using the shortcut: **Left Alt + Left Shift + Print Screen**.

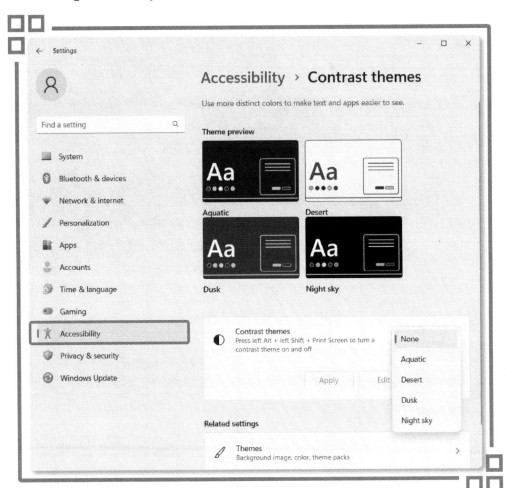

Customizing the Touch Keyboard

The touch keyboard in Windows 11 is redesigned for touch-capable devices, featuring customizable options for a more personalized experience. This includes:

- Adjustable size and theme.
- Enhanced layout, emoji panel with GIFs.
- Clipboard integration.

Customization is accessible via **Settings > Personalization > Text input > Touch keyboard**. Themes range from Light, Dark to Color Pop, with the ability to create a custom theme including key text color, background color, and even a personal image as the keyboard background.

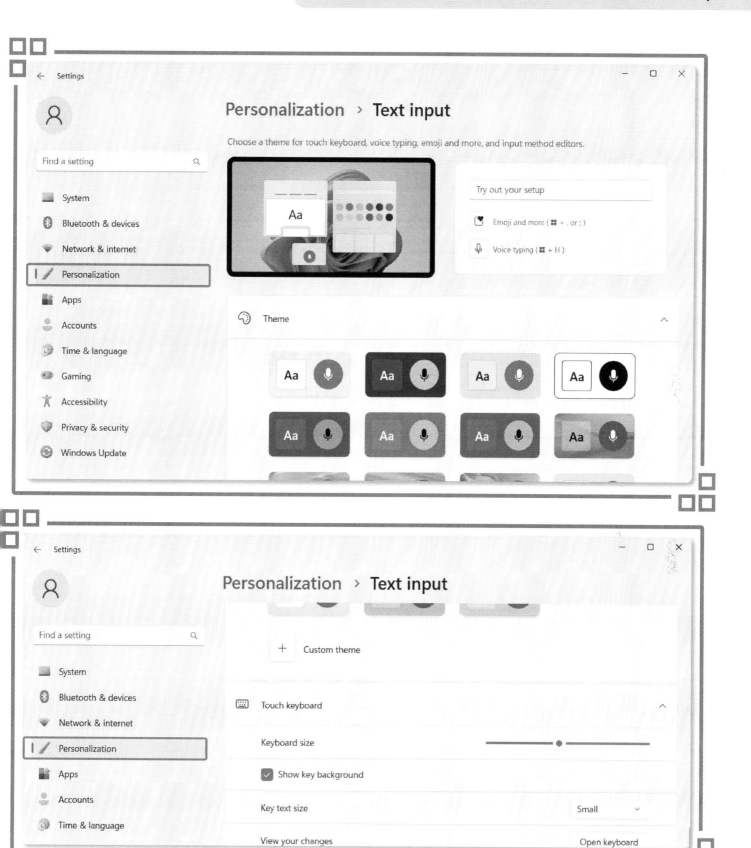

Adjusting Fonts

While the default font, Segoe, remains unchangeable, text size can be easily modified to improve readability across applications and windows. Adjust text size in **Settings > Accessibility > Text size**.

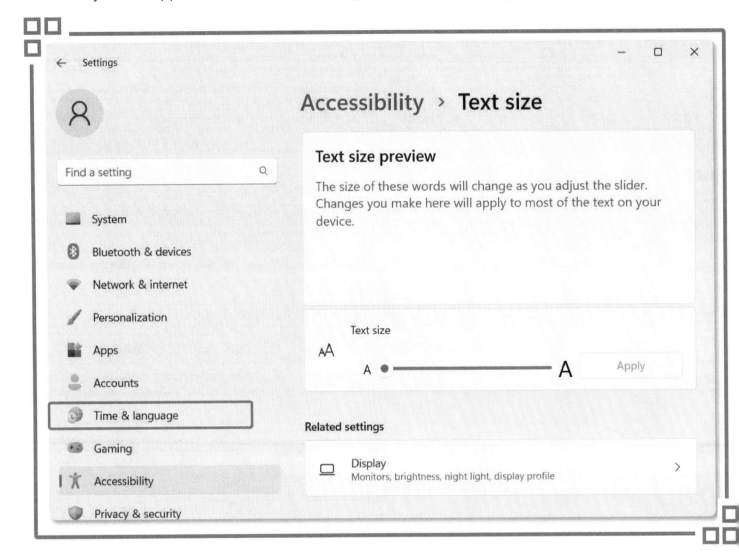

Managing Visual Effects

To mitigate distractions or discomfort from animations, Windows 11 allows users to disable or adjust visual effects like scrollbars visibility, transparency, and animation effects. These settings are available under **Settings > Accessibility > Visual effects**.

Optimizing Touch and Mouse Pointer Visibility

Enhancing the visibility and customization of the mouse pointer and touch indicator is crucial for ease of use:

- Modify pointer style and size in **Settings > Accessibility > Mouse pointer and touch**.

- Adjust touch indicator size and color for better visibility on touch-screen devices.

- Mouse sensitivity, or "mouse speed," helps in navigating the screen more efficiently, accessible via **Settings > Bluetooth & devices > Mouse**. Here, you can also switch the primary mouse button and adjust scrolling preferences to suit your needs.

These accessibility features in Windows 11 are designed to make computing more inclusive and adaptable, catering specifically to the needs of senior users or anyone requiring additional visual or navigational support.

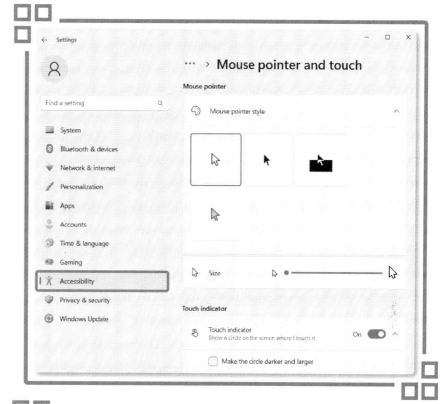

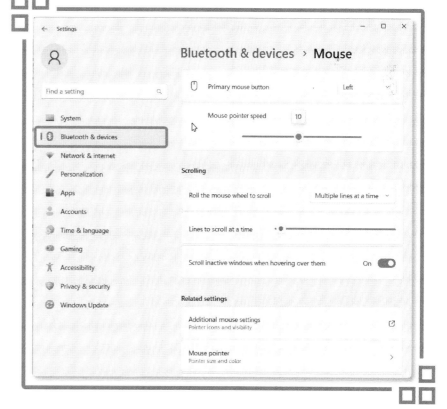

Utilizing Color Filters in Windows 11 for Enhanced Visibility

Windows 11 includes a variety of color filters designed to assist individuals with color blindness or visual impairments in better viewing the elements on their screens. To access these filters:

1) Go to **Settings > Accessibility > Color filters**.

2) Here, you'll encounter a color filter preview showcasing a color wheel, an image, and some color scales for easy understanding of how each filter modifies screen content.

Windows 11 offers several types of color filters:

- **Grayscale**: Converts the display into shades of gray, reducing visual stress and improving readability.

- **Inverted Grayscale**: Inverts the grayscale colors, providing a different contrast option.

- **Inverted Color**: Inverts all colors on the screen, offering high contrast for certain visual impairments.

- **Red-Green Filter (Deuteranopia)**: Adjusts colors to accommodate those with difficulty distinguishing between red and green hues.

- **Red-Green Filter (Protanopia)**: Similar to the Deuteranopia filter but tailored for individuals with weak red vision.

- **Blue-Yellow Filter (Tritanopia)**: Tailored for those who have difficulty distinguishing between blue and yellow shades.

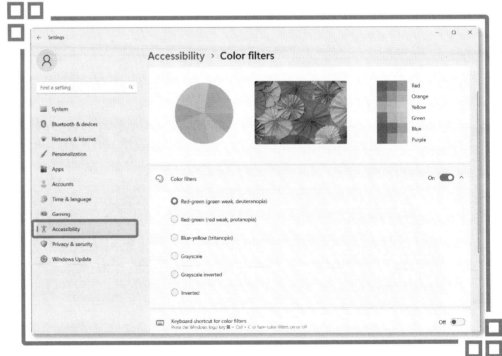

These filters are part of Windows 11's commitment to accessibility, ensuring all users can comfortably use their devices regardless of visual challenges.

Chapter 4:

Exploring Your Desktop in Windows 11

The desktop serves as the command center for your computer's activities, prominently featuring the taskbar and Start menu. The Start menu is accessible via the Windows icon, while the taskbar is the home base for application shortcuts.

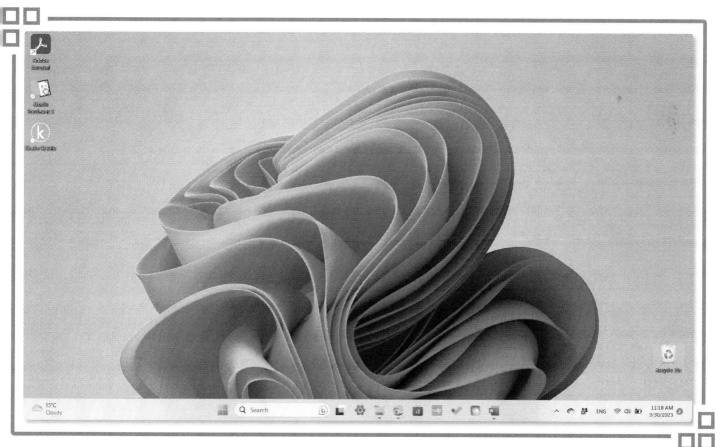

Understanding Desktop Functionality

Adjusting Time and Date

To update the time and date:

1) Right-click on the clock in the taskbar corner.
2) Select **"Adjust date and time"** from the pop-up menu to access settings in the Settings app.
3) Opt for **"Set time automatically"** to synchronize your PC with online data. Regular synchronization ensures your computer's timekeeping is accurate.

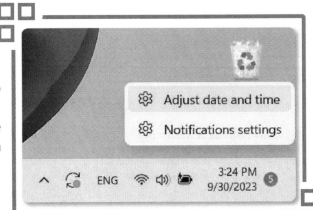

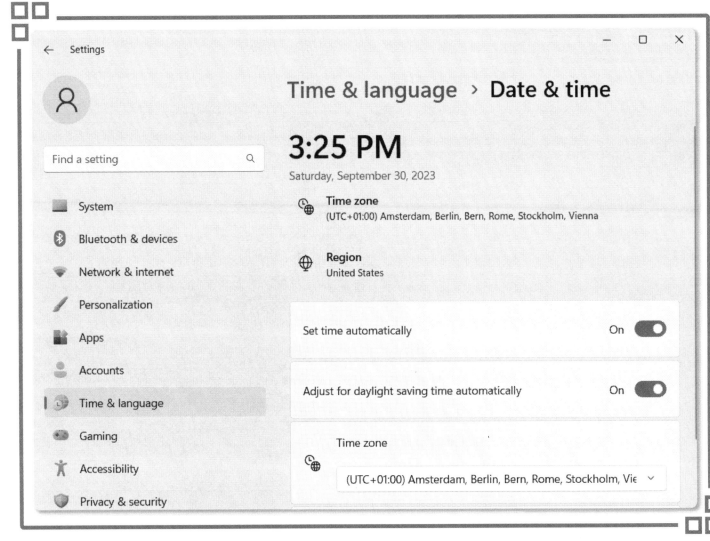

Windows Management Moving and Resizing

- **Moving**: Click and drag the Title bar at the top of any window to reposition it on your desktop.

- **Resizing**: Hover over a window's edge until the cursor changes to a double-sided arrow icon, then click and drag to adjust the window's size. The corners of the window can be manipulated similarly.

- **Maximizing and Minimizing**: Dragging the Title bar to the top of your desktop maximizes the window. To minimize, click and drag the maximized window's Title bar downwards.

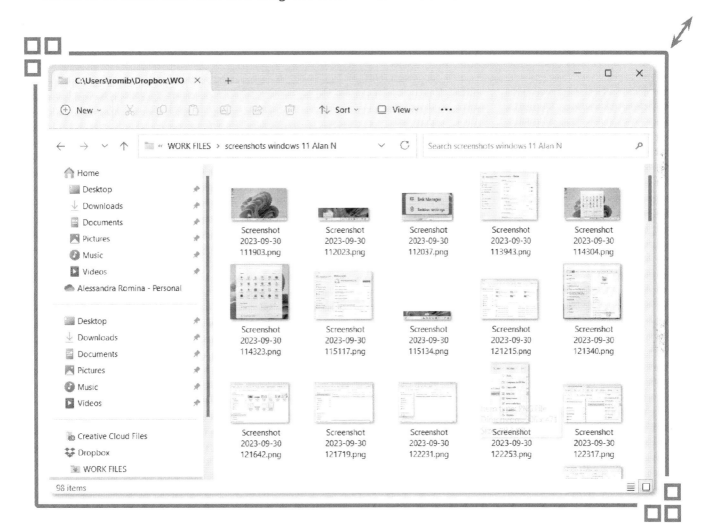

Resizing Windows with Title Bar Buttons

- The **minimize button** (a horizontal line) hides the window from view, though it remains open. Reopen it by clicking its icon in the taskbar.

- **Maximize/Restore** and **Close** buttons alongside the minimize button further control window size and closure.

Snapping Tool (Screenshoot Tool)

Windows 11 introduces the **Snap Windows** feature, enhancing multitasking:

Hover over the maximize button (or the second button from the right on the Title bar) to see layout options like side-by-side or grid patterns.

Hover over a layout choice to organize your active windows according to the selected pattern.

Enable or disable Snap Windows via **Settings > System > Multitasking > Snap Windows**, tailoring window management to your workflow preferences.

These desktop management and customization features in Windows 11 streamline your interaction with the operating system, fostering a more productive and personalized computing environment.

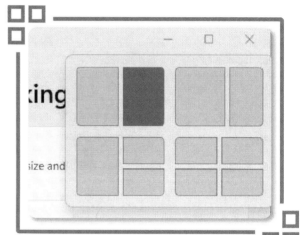

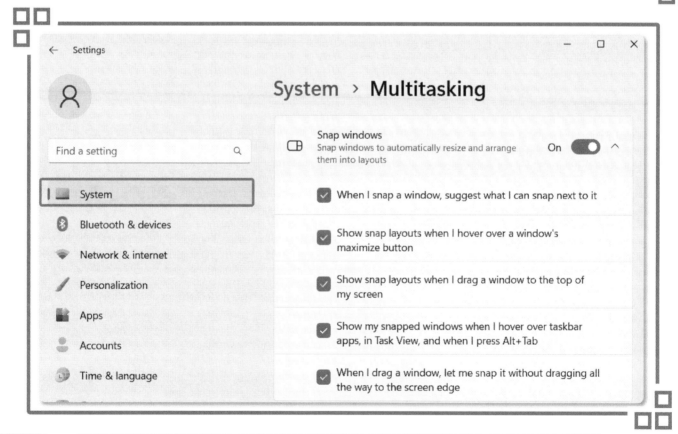

Taking Screenshots A Snapshot of Your Screen

Capturing a screenshot in Windows 11 is straightforward.

Press the **PrtSc (Print Screen)** button to capture your entire desktop to the clipboard, then paste the screenshot into an application that supports images, such as Microsoft Word or Paint 3D, using **Ctrl+V**.

For capturing just an active window, **Alt+PrtSc** is your shortcut.

The **Snipping Tool** offers more flexibility for screenshots:

- Find it by searching in the Start menu.

- It features modes like **Rectangle, Window, Full-screen,** and **Free-form** for various capture types.

- Use **Windows + Shift + S** for a quick snip, with options to edit and save the screenshot.

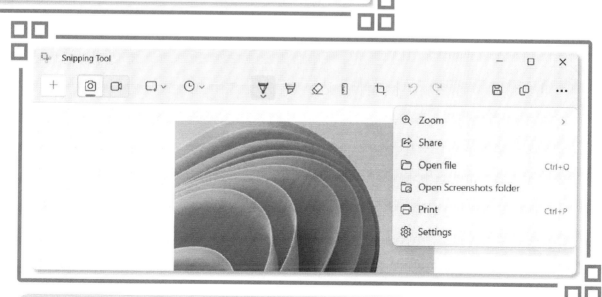

Creating Multiple Desktops Expanding Your Workspace

Windows 11 allows for multiple desktops, enhancing productivity:

1) Access this feature via the **Desktop icon** on your taskbar.

2) Click the **plus sign (+)** to add a new desktop.

3) To move windows between desktops, right-click the window's title bar and drag it to your preferred desktop.

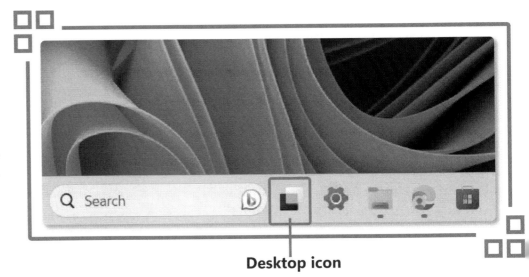

Desktop icon

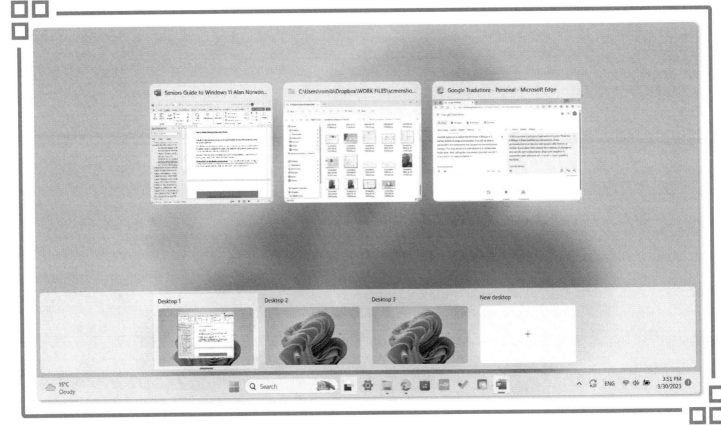

Switching Between Apps Seamless Navigation

With **Alt+Tab**, cycle through open applications. A visual overlay will display all open windows, letting you choose the one you need.

Win+Tab opens Task View, showing all open applications for easy navigation.

Mastering Task Manager Optimizing Performance

Task Manager is crucial for monitoring and managing your system's processes:

- Access it through **Ctrl+Alt+Delete**, **Ctrl+Shift+Esc**, the Start menu, or **Windows+R** then typing 'taskmgr'.

- It displays resource usage across **Processes**, real-time **Performance** metrics, **App History**, **Startup** programs, **Users**, **Details**, and **Services**.

- To close a frozen app, select it under Processes and click **End Task**.

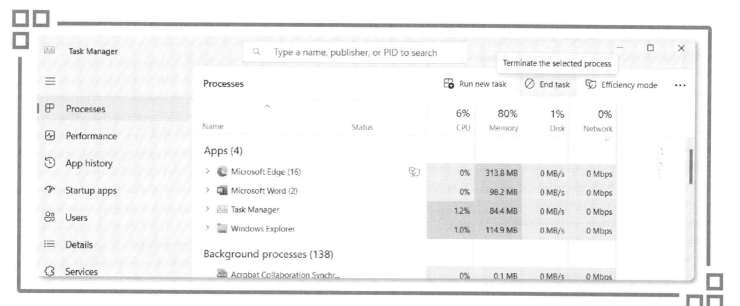

Navigating the Task Manager in Windows 11

The Task Manager in Windows 11 is a powerful tool for monitoring and managing your computer's resources and applications. On its left side, you'll find a Navigation pane categorized into several sections for detailed system analysis:

- **Processes**: This tab shows the resource usage of your applications and background processes, detailing CPU, GPU, memory, disk, and network consumption.

- **Performance**: Here, you'll see real-time graphs depicting the resource utilization for different components of your system.

- **App History**: This section allows you to review the network and CPU resources consumed by Store apps over time.

- **Startup**: Lists all the applications set to run automatically upon startup, enabling you to manage which apps load when you turn on your PC.

- **Users**: Displays resource consumption by different user accounts on the computer.

- **Details**: Provides in-depth information about the running applications and processes.

- **Services**: Shows background processes essential for running applications on your PC.

Managing Unresponsive Applications

If an application becomes unresponsive or frozen:

1) Go to the **Processes** tab, select the problematic application, and click **End Task** at the bottom right to force it to close.

2) Alternatively, right-click the application and select **"End task"** for immediate termination.

Simplifying Task Manager View

The **"Fewer options"** button at the bottom left allows you to simplify the Task Manager view, showing only active applications and hiding background activities. This streamlined view helps focus on currently running programs and provides a quicker way to close them if necessary.

Optimizing Startup Applications

To improve your computer's startup time:

1) Navigate to **Startup** applications.

2) Review the list for any unnecessary applications that auto-start. Right-click on such apps and select **'Disable'** to prevent them from running at startup.

Ensure you do not disable essential Microsoft system or hardware applications, identifiable by the **Microsoft Corporation** label under Publisher, as this could impact system functionality.

The Task Manager is a versatile feature in Windows 11, offering comprehensive insight into your system's performance and resource management, allowing for better control over your computing environment.

Chapter 5:

Application Setup Guide in Windows 11

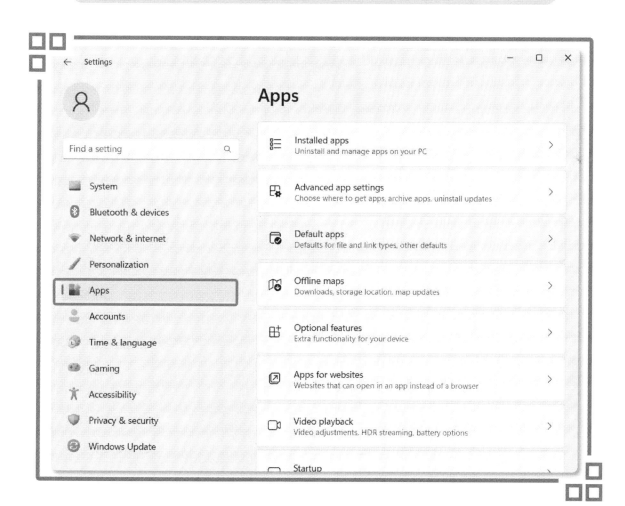

Installing Google Chrome

While Windows 11 comes equipped with Microsoft Edge, you might prefer using Google Chrome for your internet activities. Here's how to install it:

1) Open Microsoft Edge and navigate to **google.com/chrome.**

2) Alternatively, search for **"Google Chrome" using the search bar**, and click on the first result to reach the download page.

3) Click on the **download button,** accept the terms, and proceed with the installation.

After downloading, locate the installer in the Downloads folder through File Explorer and double-click to start the installation. You'll be prompted to create a desktop shortcut and a taskbar icon. If you prefer not to have these shortcuts, simply uncheck the corresponding options during the installation process.

Setting Google Chrome as Your Default Browser

Designating a default browser ensures that it opens automatically whenever you click an online link. To set Google Chrome or any other browser as your default in Windows 11:

1) Go to **Settings** > **Applications** > **Default Applications**.

2) Search for 'Edge' to find all links and file types currently set to open by default with Edge.

3) For each link and file type, change the default program to Google Chrome by clicking on them and confirming your choice.

By following these steps, you can easily install Google Chrome and set it as your default browser, tailoring your Windows 11 experience to your browsing preferences.

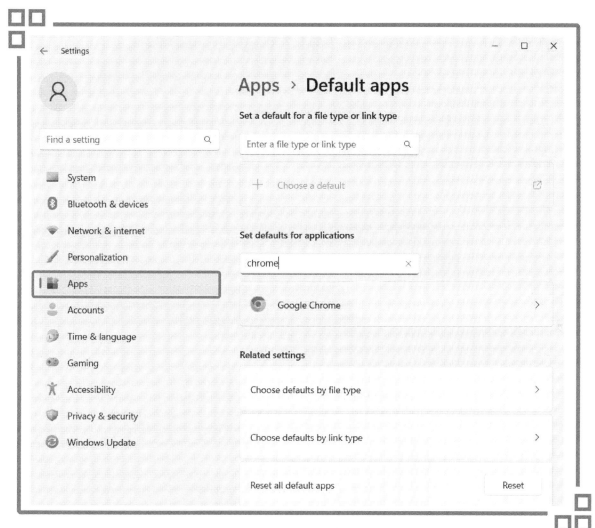

Installing Software on Your Windows 11 PC

To equip your Windows 11 computer with your desired software, start by navigating the web through a browser like Google Chrome. The software universe is vast, encompassing categories such as **antivirus programs, web browsers, VPN services, productivity suites, media players, photo and video editing tools, PC maintenance utilities, email platforms, data backup solutions, file organization tools, and social media apps**.

Below are some highly recommended and reliable software options for each category:

CATEGORY	RECOMMENDED SOFTWARE
Antiviruses	Avira Antivirus, Kaspersky Internet Security, Norton 360
Browsers	Google Chrome, Microsoft Edge, Mozilla Firefox
VPN Services	NordVPN, Express VPN
Productivity/Office	Microsoft Office 365, Google Suite, Apache Open Office
Media Players	VLC Media Player, GOM Player, MediaPlayer Classic
Photo and Video Editors	Adobe Creative Suite, Canva (Webapp), Clip Studio Paint
PC Repair Tools	Wise Registry Cleaner
Email Clients	Microsoft Outlook, Gmail (Webapp)
File Management	Total Commander, Directory Opus, File Viewer Plus
Social	Zoom, Teams, Skype

Finding and Downloading Software

1) To locate software, type its name along with **"download"** into your **browser's search bar.**

2) Always opt for the link directing you to the developer's official site to ensure legitimacy.

3) Note that many programs, like **Microsoft Office 365** and various **Adobe products**, may require payment before downloading. Follow the provided instructions post-payment for downloading and installation.

4) Check your PC's compatibility by reviewing the software's system requirements on the developer's site.

5) Once compatible, proceed with the download, accepting any terms and conditions, then start the installation process by following simple prompts.

Installing VLC Media Player

A highly recommended free app for media playback is **VLC Media Player**.

1) Visit **videolan.org/vlc/index.html** or search "Download VLC" to find the Videolan website.

2) Click "Download VLC". After downloading, locate the file and double-click to begin installation.

3) You'll encounter a prompt asking for permission to make changes to your device. Follow the steps for language selection and installation location. VLC will then be accessible from the Start menu.

4) To set VLC as your default media player, go to **Settings > System > Programs > Default programs**.

Installing Norton Antivirus

Enhance your Windows 11 security with Norton Antivirus. Ensure your PC meets these requirements:

- **2 GB RAM**

- **300 MB** of free disk space for download

- **1.3 GB** of free disk space for installation

- An internet connection

Purchase a license from **https://it.norton.com/products,** create a Norton account, download, and install the software following the provided instructions.

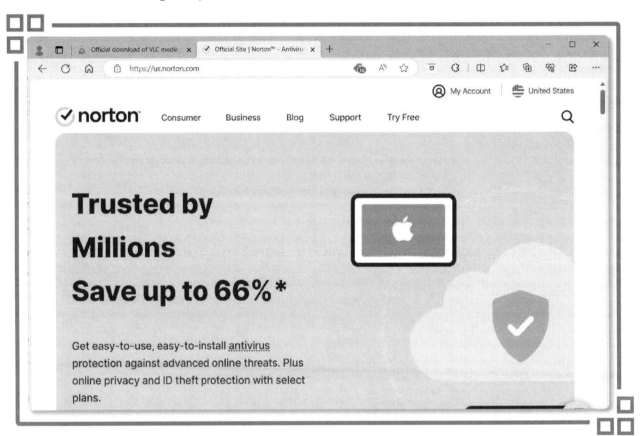

Installing WhatsApp Messenger

Stay connected with WhatsApp Desktop, easily synced with your mobile app for seamless messaging:

1) Open the **Microsoft Store** from the taskbar or Start menu.

2) Search for **"WhatsApp Desktop"** and click the 'Free' button to download and install.

These instructions guide you through downloading and setting up Google Chrome, VLC Media Player, Norton Antivirus, and WhatsApp Messenger, enhancing your Windows 11 experience with essential internet, media, security, and communication tools.

Setting Up Zoom on Windows 11

Zoom is a popular video conferencing tool that allows for easy setup of video calls with friends, family, or colleagues. It stands out for its effectiveness and user-friendliness among similar platforms.

Installation Guide:

1) Navigate to zoom.us/download.

2) Click the **Download** button for the Zoom client for meetings.

3) Find the installer in your **Downloads** folder and double-click it.

4) A prompt asking, "Do you want to allow this app to make changes to your device?" will appear. Select **Yes**.

Follow the brief setup instructions, and Zoom will be installed and ready for use.

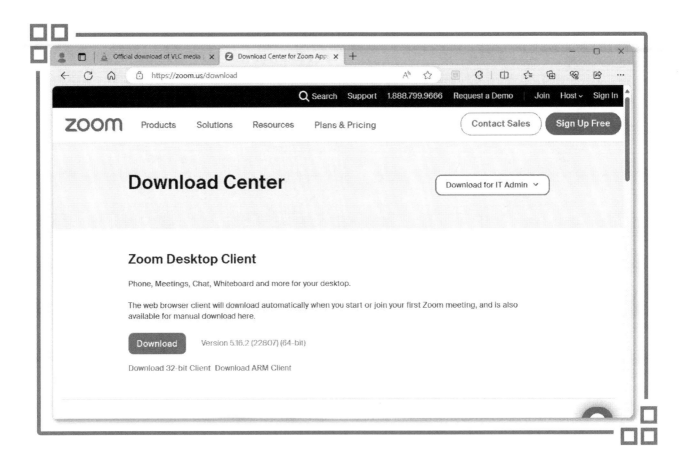

Important Considerations for Software Installation

- **User Permission**: Windows 11 will ask for your permission before allowing any app to make changes to your device. Ensure you proceed only with software from trusted sources. Researching a program's reliability online can provide useful insights.

- **Review Permissions Carefully**: It's crucial to carefully read through all permissions requested by the software. Refrain from agreeing to unnecessary terms or conditions. Be wary of software asking for access to unrelated features or data, like a calendar app requesting access to your media. Always uncheck options that are not essential for the software's functionality.

These steps and considerations will help you safely install Zoom and other software on Windows 11, ensuring both a secure and efficient experience.

Chapter 6:

Backup and Restore:
Keep Your Memories and Documents

In today's digital realm, our data—photos, documents, contacts, and emails—are invaluable. The risk of losing these to hardware failure or accidents underscores the importance of regular data backups, akin to keeping photocopies of crucial documents in a safe place.

Backing Up Your Data

1) **Identify Important Data**: Determine the data you need to safeguard —this might include photos, documents, emails, and contacts.

2) **Select a Backup Location**: Options for backup storage include external hard drives, USB sticks, or cloud services like OneDrive, Google Drive, or Dropbox.

3) **Execute the Backup**: Utilize the built-in backup programs on many computers to regularly back up your selected data.

Restoring Data from Backups

1) **Connect Your Backup Storage**: If using physical storage like an external hard drive or USB, connect it to your computer.

2) **Utilize Backup Software**: Employ the restoration feature in your computer's backup software.

3) **Verify Restored Files**: Ensure all intended files have been correctly restored post-process.

Using OneDrive for Automated Backups

OneDrive, Microsoft's cloud storage solution, offers automated backups:

- **Setup**: Log in with your Microsoft account and choose which folders to back up.

- **Continuous Backup**: Once set, OneDrive automatically backs up new files or edits.

- **Access Anywhere**: Log into your OneDrive account from any internet-connected device to access your files.

Choosing Between OneDrive, Google Drive, or Dropbox

The best cloud storage service depends on your needs:

- **OneDrive** is ideal for those heavily invested in Windows and Office ecosystems.

- **Google Drive** excels for users integrated into Google's ecosystem, including Gmail and Google Workspace.

- **Dropbox** is recognized for its simplicity and reliability, making it great for file sharing across different platforms.

Setting Up OneDrive

To use OneDrive for backups:

1) **Website Access**: Go to **https://onedrive.live.com** and sign in or create a Microsoft account.

2) **Install OneDrive App**: Download and install the OneDrive app for your operating system.

3) **Select Folders for Backup**: Choose which folders to sync during setup, with options to customize.

4) **Automatic Syncing**: OneDrive will sync the selected folders with the cloud, with manual options available for other files.

5) **Verification**: Regularly check the OneDrive app to ensure files are synced correctly.

Key Considerations for Using OneDrive

- **Storage Limits**: As of my last update, OneDrive offers a base of 5GB free storage, with options to purchase more.

- **Internet Connection**: A stable internet connection is crucial for syncing, especially for large data volumes.

By following these steps, you can ensure your precious data is backed up and restorable, offering peace of mind against data loss.

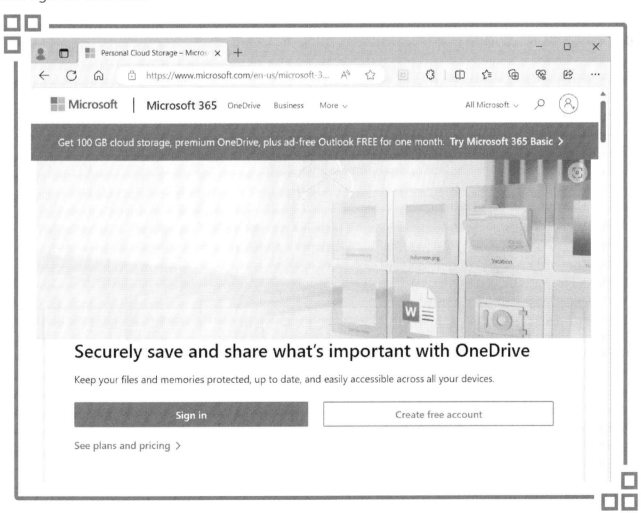

Chapter 7:

Master Web Navigation on Windows 11

Introduction to Web Browsers

In the realm of web navigation, Microsoft Edge and Google Chrome stand as the foremost choices for internet browsing. While both browsers offer similar functionalities, this chapter will delve into how to utilize them for essential online activities.

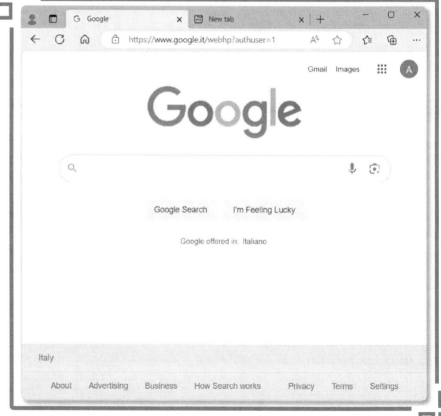

Exploring Browser Functions

Both Edge and Chrome are equipped with numerous features to enhance your web browsing experience.

Navigating Microsoft Edge:

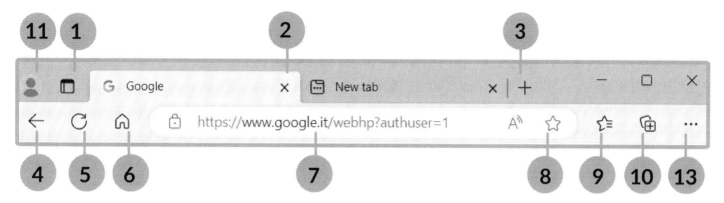

1) **Tab Actions Menu**: Explore recently closed tabs and more.
2) **Close Current Tab**: Exit the active tab.
3) **Open New Tab**: Initiate a fresh browsing tab.
4) **Back**: Navigate to the previous page.
5) **Forward**: Move to the next page.
6) **Reload**: Refresh the current webpage.
7) **Home**: Visit your homepage with a single click.
8) **Address Bar**: Enter URLs or search terms here.
9) **Favorites**: Bookmark your favorite pages.
10) **View Favorites**: Access your bookmarked sites.
11) **Reading Lists**: Utilize "Add to a collection" to save pages for later.
12) **Profile Access**: Check your account and profile details.
13) **Additional Tools**: Explore more browser functionalities.

Navigating Google Chrome:

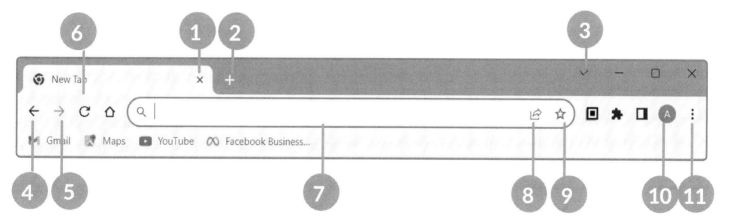

1) **Close Active Tab**: Terminate the current tab.
2) **New Tab**: Start a new browsing session.
3) **Recently Opened/Closed Tabs**: Access a history of your tabs.

4) **Go Back**: Return to a previous page (Tip: Holding the back button reveals a drop-down menu for direct navigation to earlier pages).

5) **Forward**: Proceed to the next page.

6) **Reload**: Refresh the current page.

7) **Address Bar**: For typing in web addresses or search queries.

8) **Share Page**: Options include creating shareable links, emailing the page, generating QR codes, casting to devices, and direct sharing on social platforms like Twitter and LinkedIn.

9) **Bookmark**: Save pages for easy access.

10) **Profile Access**: View your account and profile information.

11) **Additional Tools**: Discover more features to optimize your browsing.

Both Microsoft Edge and Google Chrome offer a comprehensive set of tools for efficient web navigation, ensuring a seamless online experience. Whether you're bookmarking favorite sites, managing tabs, or sharing content, these browsers cater to a wide range of browsing preferences.

Understanding Tabs in Web Browsing

Tabs in internet browsers enable you to open multiple web pages within a single window, helping keep your desktop from getting cluttered. Located above the address bar, tabs are easily identifiable and navigable. To open a new tab, simply click the + sign next to the currently active tab.

Right-clicking any link offers the option to **"Open in new tab"** for multitasking or **"Open in new window"** for separate browsing sessions, enhancing your online experience by allowing simultaneous access to various sites.

Adding a Bookmark

Microsoft Edge:

Bookmarks allow you to save and store the URL of a website for easy future access. Here's how to bookmark a page in **Microsoft Edge:**

1) Navigate to the desired website.

2) On the toolbar, locate and select the **Star** button on the right.

3) Click the star button with the + symbol to add to "Favorites."

4) The website's name will appear; hit **Enter** to save.

5) For organizational purposes, you can rename the website or sort it into folders and subfolders.

6) Alternatively, quickly bookmark a page by pressing **Ctrl+D**.

Bookmarks streamline your browsing by enabling quick access to frequently visited sites, thereby saving time and enhancing productivity.

Bookmarking in Google Chrome

To save your favorite websites in Google Chrome:

1) Navigate to the website you wish to bookmark.

2) Click the **Star icon** on the right side of the toolbar.

3) Choose the desired folder and website name for saving.

4) Press **Enter** to save your bookmark.

5) Use the **Ctrl+D** keyboard shortcut to quickly add a website to your Bookmarks. For better organization, you may rename the site and sort bookmarks into folders and subfolders.

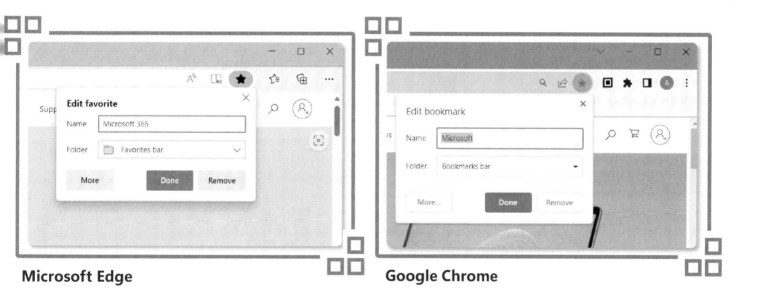

Microsoft Edge   **Google Chrome**

Displaying the Bookmarks Bar

The bookmarks bar offers quick access to your saved sites and folders.

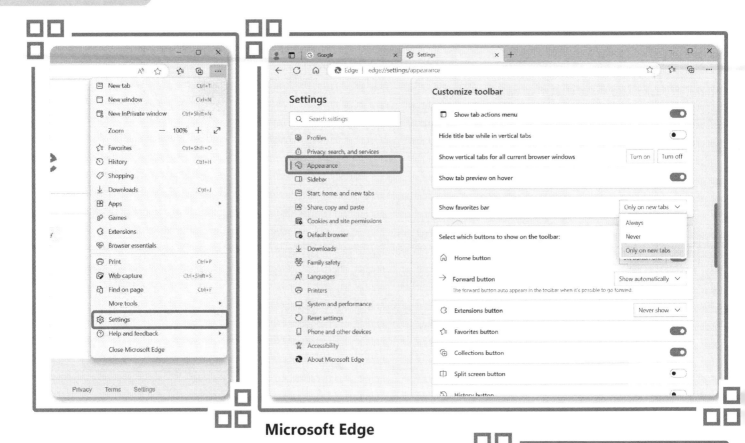

Microsoft Edge

In Microsoft Edge:

1) Click the **Tools button** and select **Settings > Appearance > Customize the toolbar > Show favorites bar**.

2) Choose **"Always"** or **"Only on new tabs"** to display the favorites bar.

3) Alternatively, toggle the favorites bar visibility with **Ctrl + Shift + B**.

In Google Chrome:

1) Click the **Tools button** and navigate to **Settings > Appearance** and enable **Show bookmarks bar**.

2) Toggle this setting to display the bookmarks bar.

3) Use **Ctrl + Shift + B** to quickly show or hide the bookmarks bar.

Google Chrome

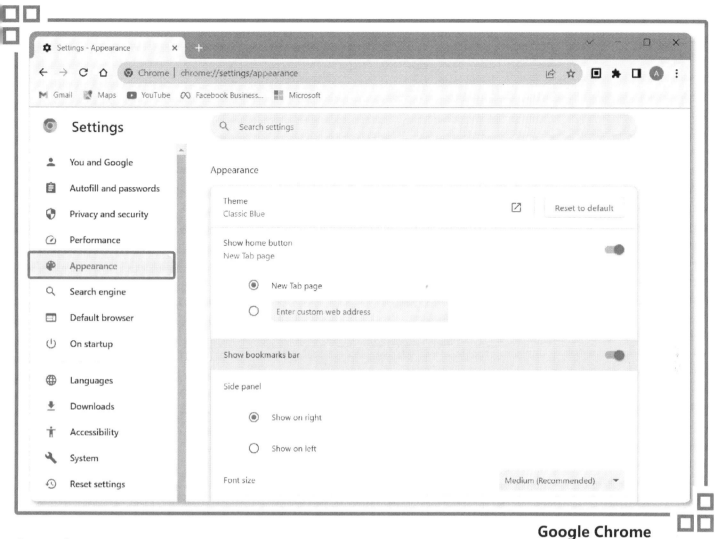

Google Chrome

Setting Up a New Homepage

Customize your browser's startup page to open your preferred site or a new tab.

In Google Chrome:

1) Go to **Settings** and select **Appearance**.
2) Enable **"Show Home button"**.
3) Choose to open a **New Tab Page** or a specific **URL** as your homepage.

In Microsoft Edge:

1) Under **Settings > Appearance**, select **Customize toolbar**.
2) Enable the **"Home button"** and select **"Set button URL"**.
3) Configure the homepage settings to open a new tab or a specific URL.

These steps will guide you through bookmarking sites, accessing the bookmarks bar for quick navigation, and setting up a custom homepage in both Google Chrome and Microsoft Edge, enhancing your web browsing experience.

Viewing and Deleting Browsing History

Your web browser records all your visited websites, allowing you to revisit pages, delete specific entries, or clear your history entirely.

Google Chrome:

1) Access **History** by clicking the Tools button.
2) Review websites visited in the last 90 days. Click on a page to revisit it.
3) To delete history, open the History tab or press **Ctrl+H**.
4) Select specific entries to delete or use "Clear browsing data" to remove all history.

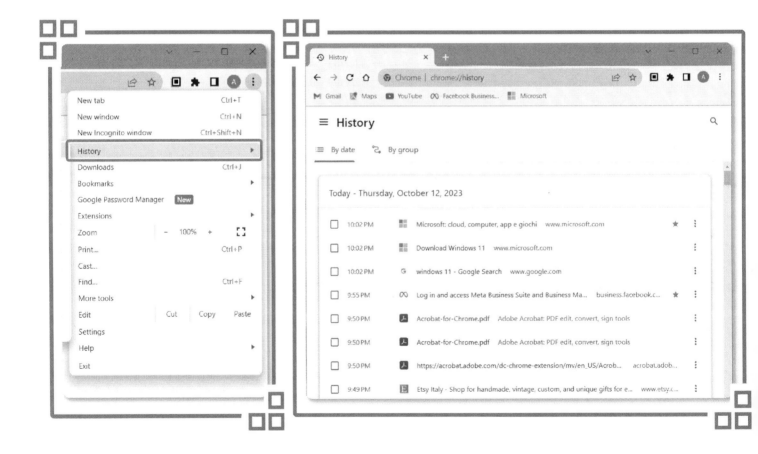

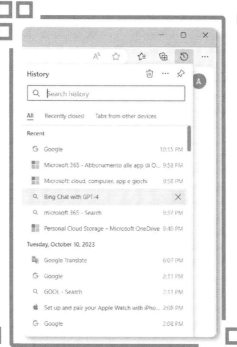

Microsoft Edge:

1) Access **History** from the Tools button. Review recent visits.
2) Hover over an entry and click the **X** to delete it.
3) To clear all history, click the three horizontal dots > "Clear browsing data".
4) For detailed browsing data, including time and date, select "Open history page" from the History window's menu.

Activating Private Browsing

Private browsing modes prevent saving your browsing history and other data on your device or account, though your ISP may still access your network activity.

Microsoft Edge - InPrivate Browsing:

Click the three horizontal dots > "New InPrivate Window", or press **Ctrl+Shift+N**.

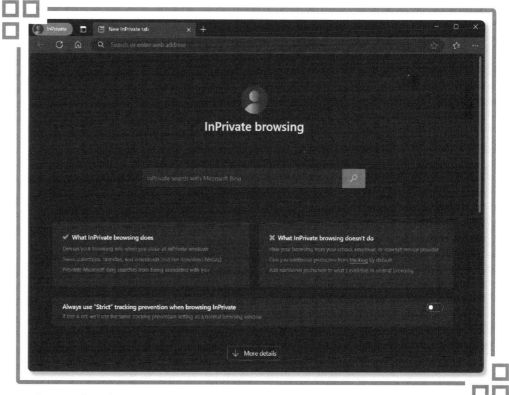

Microsoft Edge

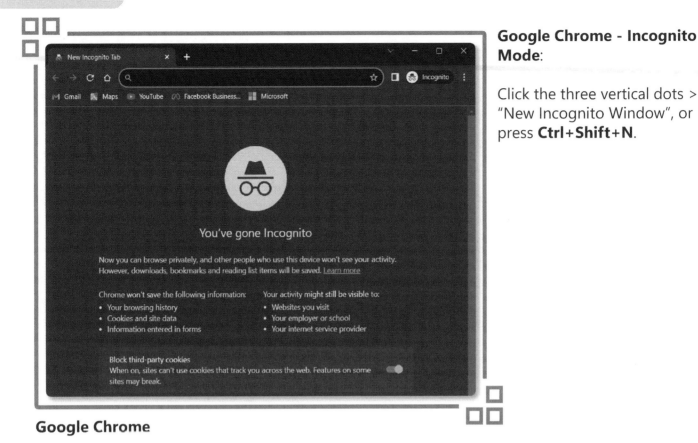

Google Chrome - Incognito Mode:

Click the three vertical dots > "New Incognito Window", or press **Ctrl+Shift+N**.

Google Chrome

How to Enlarge a Page

Zooming in or out on a webpage can improve readability or fit more content on your screen.

In both Microsoft Edge and Google Chrome:

1) Click the three vertical dots in the top right.
2) Select **"Zoom"** and use the + or - to adjust.
3) Alternatively, zoom with the mouse wheel while holding the **Ctrl** key.

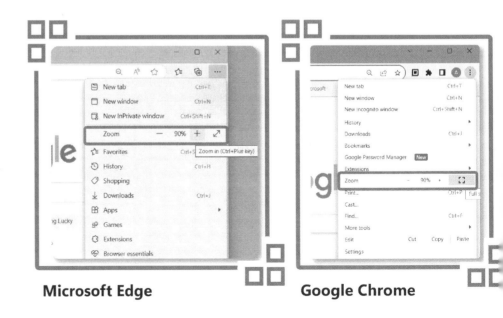

Microsoft Edge   **Google Chrome**

How to Block Ads and Manage Pop-ups in Your Web Browser

Dealing with intrusive pop-up ads can be frustrating, but your web browser offers ways to control them.

Microsoft Edge:

1) Navigate to **Settings > Cookies and site permissions > Pop-ups and redirects**.
2) Ensure this feature is enabled to block unwanted pop-ups.
3) Customize settings to allow or block pop-ups from specific sites by adding their URLs.

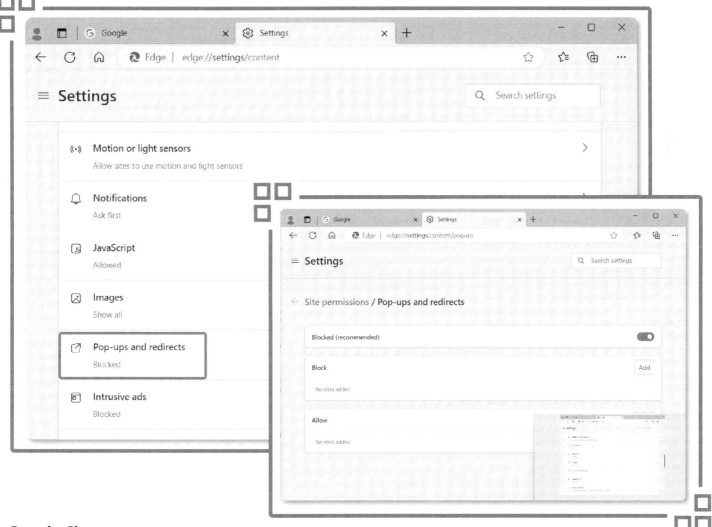

Google Chrome:

1) Access **Settings > Security and Privacy > Site settings**.
2) Under "**Default behavior,**" ensure "**Don't allow sites to send pop-ups or use redirects**" is checked.
3) Further refine by adding URLs of sites to allow or block pop-ups.

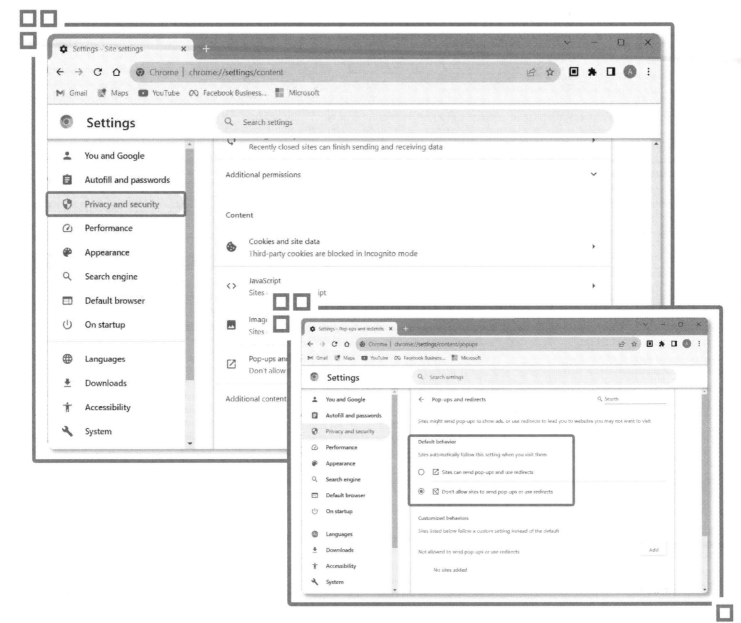

Enhancing Productivity with Right-Click Options

Right-clicking an image or link in your browser opens a menu with various useful options.

In Microsoft Edge:

- **"Open image in a new tab"**: Displays the image with its URL in the address bar.
- **"Save image/link as"**: Opens File Explorer for saving the image/link.
- **"Copy image"** or **"Copy link"**: Copies the item to your clipboard.
- **"Copy image link"**: Copies the image URL to your clipboard.
- **"Create a QR Code for this Image"**: Generates a QR code linking to the image URL.
- **"Search the web for images"**: Finds similar images online.

- **"Search Bing in the sidebar"**: Uses Bing in a sidebar for related searches.
- **"Open in Immersive Reader"**: Offers a clean, distraction-free reading layout.
- **"Share"**: Allows sharing via email or social media.
- **"Web Capture"**: Lets you take and save screenshots.
- **"Inspect"**: View the source code of the website.

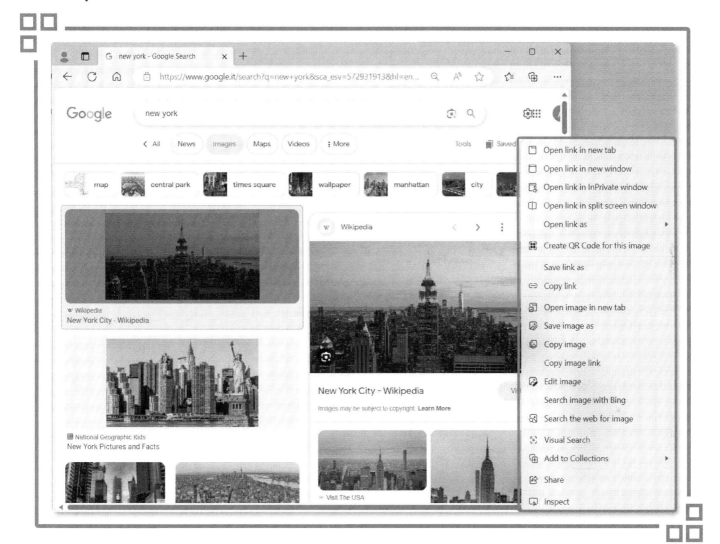

In Google Chrome:

- **"Open image/link in new tab"**: Opens the item in a new tab.
- **"Save image/link as"**: Saves the image/link to a specified location on your computer.
- **"Copy image/link"**: Copies the item to your clipboard.
- **"Copy image address"**: Copies the image's URL.
- **"Create QR Code for this Image"**: Creates a QR code for the image URL.
- **"Google Lens" image search**: Searches the web for similar images.
- **"Inspect"**: Allows viewing of the web page's source code.

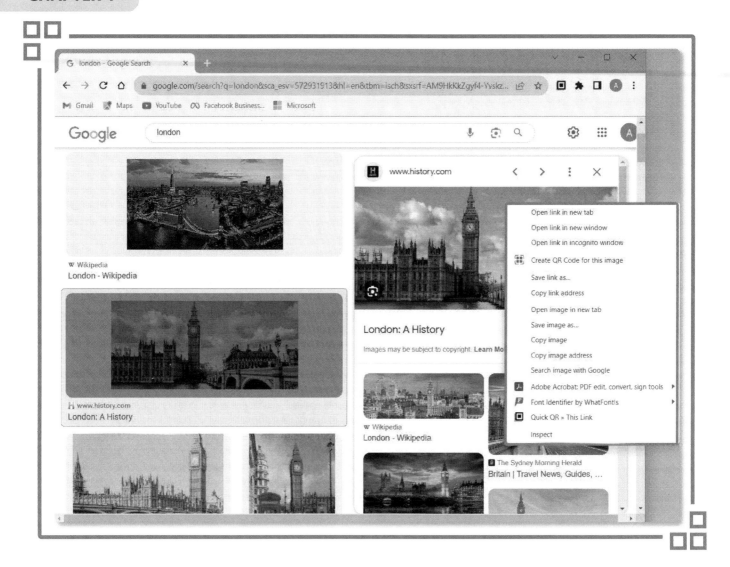

Downloading Files

While navigating the web, you may encounter content like documents or images you wish to save. Documents are often accessible for download through a link. Right-click the link and choose **"Save link as..."** to save it to your computer. This action will open File Explorer, where you can name your download and choose its destination. Similarly, images can be saved by right-clicking and selecting **"Save image as..."**, then specifying the name and storage location.

Extensions and Add-ons

Web browsers offer extensions and add-ons as tools to enrich and customize your browsing experience, represented by small icons near your address bar.

Microsoft Edge:

- Access add-ons by selecting **Extensions** from the Tools menu, where you can also manage installed extensions.

- The **Edge Add-ons page** offers various tools categorized under accessibility, productivity, entertainment, and more, including **Most Popular**, **Newest**, and **Editor's Picks**.

- Install an add-on by clicking **Get**, then **Add Extension** in the pop-up window. This action places an extension button next to your address bar.

- To use an add-on, click its icon next to the address bar. Always check ratings to gauge the add-on's effectiveness.

Google Chrome:

- Find extensions at **chrome.google.com/webstore/category/extensions**. Manage existing ones via **Tools > More tools > Extensions**.

- The **Google Web Store** lists thousands of extensions for various purposes, featuring categories like Recommended for You and Favorites of 2021.

- To install, right-click an extension and select **"Add to Chrome"**, then **Add Extension**. A new icon will appear next to your address bar for easy access.

- If no new icon appears, a puzzle-piece icon represents all your extensions. Use the pin buttons to pin or unpin extension icons to your taskbar for visibility.

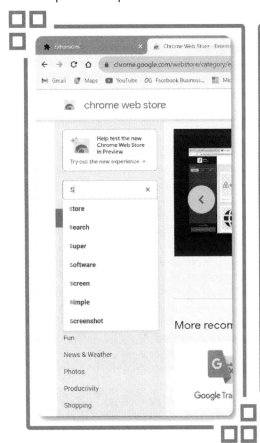

Chapter 8:

Security – Stay Safe on Web Navigation

In the digital age, safeguarding your online presence and personal data against phishing attempts is essential. Phishing, a method where attackers "fish" for victims with deceitful emails mimicking reputable sources, poses a significant risk to digital security.

Understanding Phishing's Purpose

Phishing aims to trick individuals into divulging sensitive information like passwords, credit card numbers, and social security numbers through emails that seem to be from trustworthy organizations.

Identifying Phishing Emails

- **Requests for Personal Information**: Legitimate companies rarely ask for sensitive information via email.

- **Grammatical and Spelling Errors**: Though not universal, these mistakes can be red flags.

- **Suspicious URLs**: Always hover over links to check if the URL matches the expected destination.

- **Scare Tactics**: Phishing emails often use threats or unbelievable offers to prompt action.

- **Unexpected Attachments**: Be wary of emails with attachments, which could contain malware.

Protecting Against Phishing

- **Verification**: Contact the organization directly through verified means if an email seems suspicious.

- **Email Filters**: Use your email platform's filters to help catch phishing attempts.

- **Software Updates**: Stay up to date with security patches and updates.

- **Self-Education**: Knowledge is a powerful defense. Attend webinars and read up on the latest security practices.

Empowering Security with Passwords and Password Managers

Passwords are the first line of defense against unauthorized access, yet their importance is often underestimated.

Strengthening Your Password

- **Length and Complexity**: Longer passwords with a mix of character types are more secure.

- **Personal Information**: Avoid easily guessable details like names and dates.

- **Dictionary Words**: Non-dictionary words are harder to crack.

- **Regular Changes**: Periodically changing passwords can prevent unauthorized access.

- **Password Managers**: Tools like LastPass, 1Password, and Dashlane secure and manage your passwords, requiring only one master password to access your accounts.

Boosting Security with Two-Factor Authentication (2FA)

Even strong passwords can be compromised, making 2FA an essential second layer of security.

Understanding 2FA:

- **First Factor - Something You Know**: Typically a password.

- **Second Factor - Something You Have**: A dynamic code sent to your phone or generated by an app.

Setting Up 2FA:

- **Access Security Settings**: In your account settings, find the option for 2FA.

- **Choose an Authentication Method**: Options include SMS codes, emails, or authentication apps.

- **Complete Setup**: Follow on-screen instructions to activate and verify 2FA.

Incorporating these practices into your digital routine can significantly enhance your security online, safeguarding your data and personal information from phishing and unauthorized access.

Chapter 9:

Emailing Your Friends and Family

Email communication has evolved significantly, providing multiple ways to stay in touch through either apps or web browsers.

For prompt messaging, utilizing the Mail app or another email client is a popular choice.

Native Windows 11 - Mail App

Creating a New Email Account

1) Open the Mail app from the Start menu.
2) Click on **Add account** if it's your first time; otherwise, go to **Settings > Manage Accounts**.
3) Select the account type you wish to add. Options include Outlook, Google, Yahoo, Office 365, iCloud, or POP/IMAP accounts.
4) For Google accounts with two-step verification enabled, enter the verification code received.
5) Input your login credentials and click **Done** to begin syncing your emails and contacts.

Advanced Setup

Some older email accounts might require advanced configuration. Choose **Advanced options** when prompted and enter the necessary details.

Adding Multiple Email Addresses

1) In the Mail app, navigate to **Settings > Manage Accounts > + Add Account**.
2) Follow the prompts to add and configure additional accounts.
3) To switch between accounts for sending emails, select the desired account from the navigation pane.

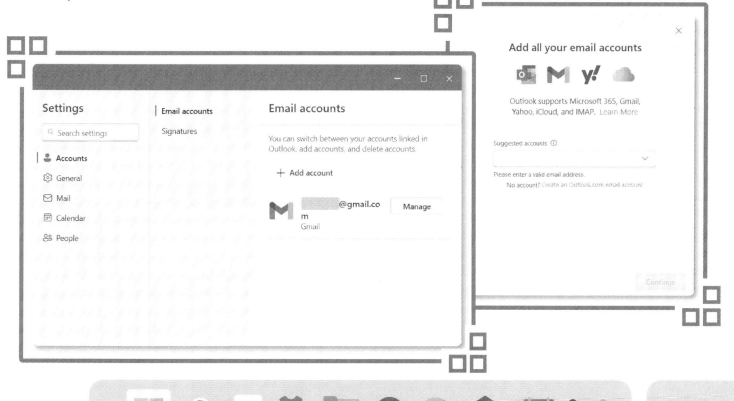

Learning to Use the Mail App

The Mail app features several navigational buttons:

- **Collapse**: Minimizes the navigation pane.
- **+ New mail**: Starts a new email draft.
- **Accounts**: Displays account information.
- **Folders**: Access to Inbox, Drafts, Sent, and Archive.
- **Switch to Calendar/Mail**: Toggles between Mail and Calendar apps.
- **Settings**: Access the app's settings.

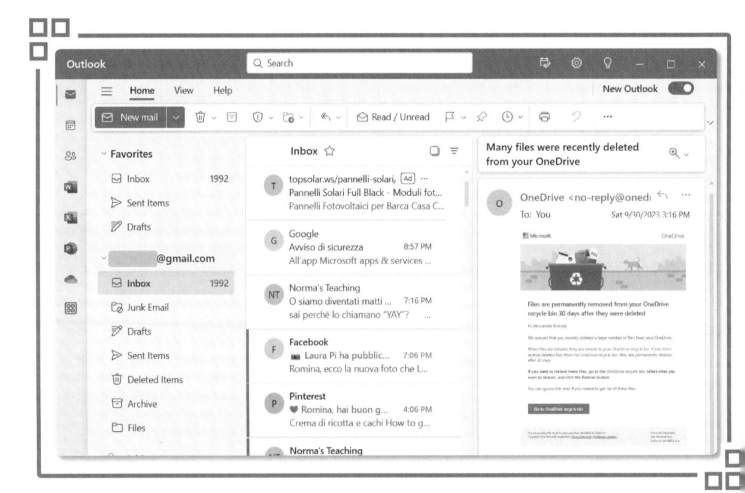

Composing Your First Email

1) Click **+ New Mail** to open the writing pane.
2) In the 'To:' field, enter the recipient's email address.
3) Use CC (carbon copy) to include secondary recipients.
4) Write a concise subject line.
5) Compose your message in the text field.

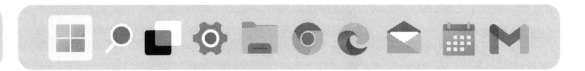

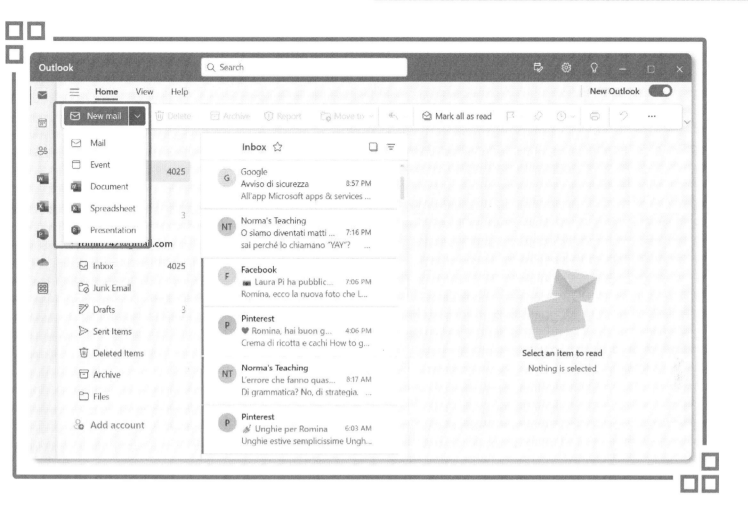

Email Formatting Options

- **Insert**: Allows adding files, images, or links.
- **Format**: Provides text formatting tools like Bold, Italics, and Lists.
- **Draw**: Enables freehand notes or doodles.
- **Options**: Offers spell check, zoom, find tools, and priority settings.

Attaching Files in the Mail App

The Mail app's **Insert** tab allows for easy attachment of files, images, tables, and links to your emails. Alternatively, you can drag and drop items directly from File Explorer into your draft to attach them.

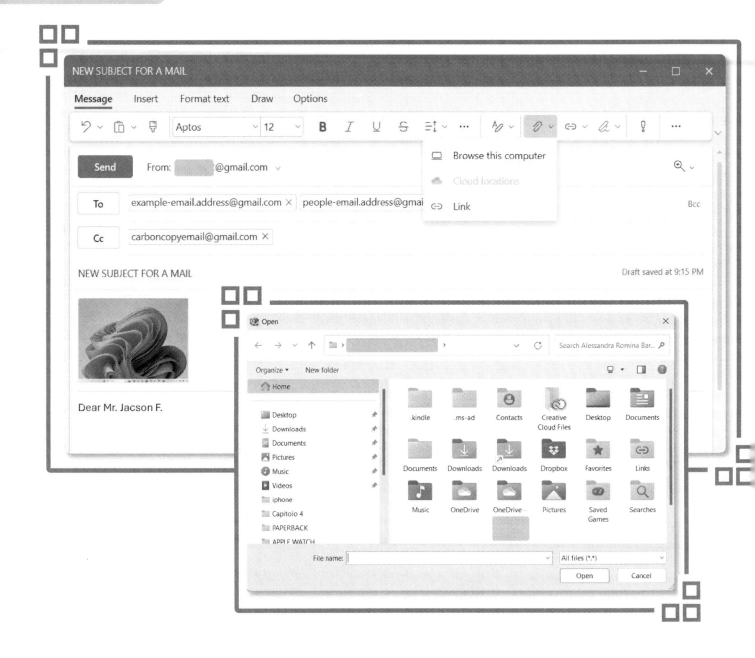

Reading and Replying to Emails

1) **Refresh**: Hit the refresh button to check for new messages.

2) **New Emails**: Look for a numerical indicator next to your Inbox or relevant folders, and click to view.

3) **Unread Messages**: These are bolded for easy identification. Click on a message in the reading pane to open it.

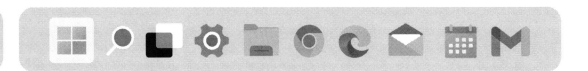

4) **Replying**: Use the 'Reply' or 'Reply all' buttons for individual or group responses, respectively. Use 'Forward' to send the message to another recipient.

5) **Managing Emails**: Options include archiving, deleting, setting flags, marking as unread, moving to different folders, or marking as spam.

6) **Additional Tools**: Tools include searching within an email, saving, printing, zooming, and opening emails in new windows for multitasking.

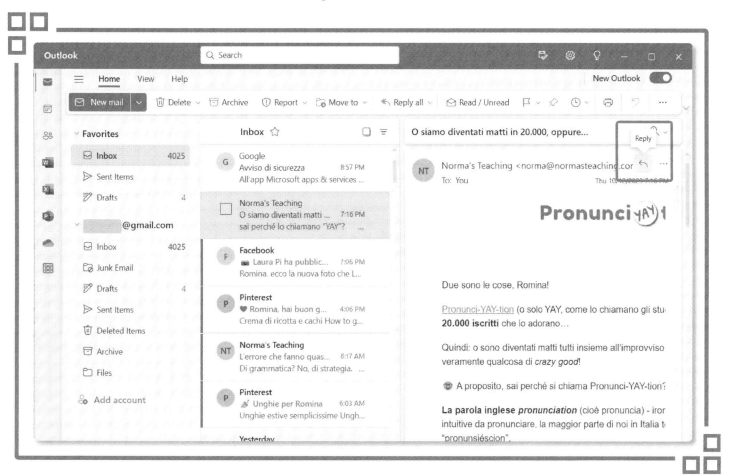

Understanding the Spam Folder

The spam folder helps keep your Inbox clean by filtering out junk mail. The Mail app automatically directs suspicious emails here, clearing the folder every 30 days. If legitimate emails are mistakenly marked as spam, you can manually move them back to the Inbox to refine the app's filtering.

Organizing and Sorting Mail

Emails are automatically sorted into folders such as Inbox, Drafts, Sent Items, Archive, Deleted Items, and Junk Email. Create personalized folders for further organization:

1) **Creating Folders**: Right-click in the navigation pane and select "Create new folder" for custom organization.

2) **Sorting**: Drag and drop folders to arrange them, or mark specific folders as Favorites for easy access.

3) **Folder Management**: Right-click a folder to rename, delete, empty, or pin it to the Start menu for quick access.

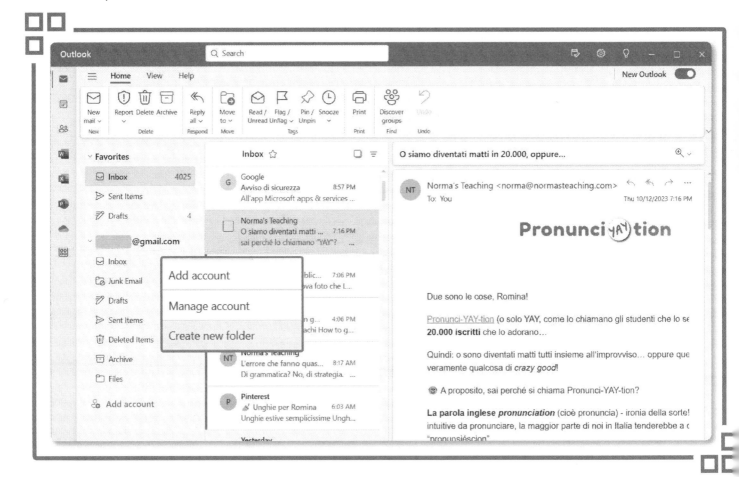

Customizing the Mail App

Personalize your email experience:

- **List Pane Customization**: Adjust swipe actions, organization, and previews in **Settings**.
- **Reading Pane**: Modify auto-open settings, marking items as read, and more.
- **Email Signature**: Create a personalized sign-off for your emails.
- **Notifications**: Customize sounds, banners, and pin folders for alerts.
- **Appearance**: Change the background image, theme, folder color, and message spacing to suit your preference.

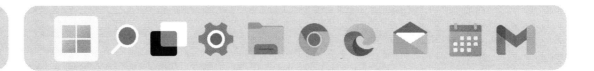

**Settings
Mail App:**

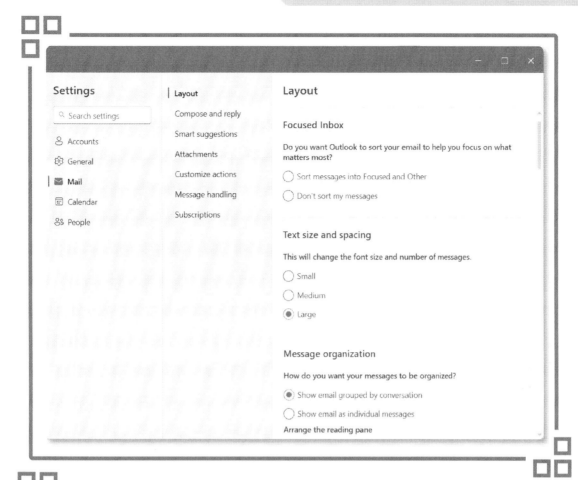

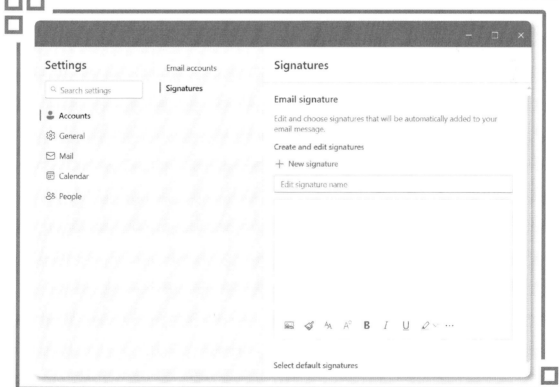

Google Mail (Gmail) - Your Gateway to Efficient Email Communication

Google Mail, widely recognized as Gmail, presents an excellent alternative for email communication, catering exclusively to Gmail addresses.

Accessing Gmail

- Navigate to **www.gmail.com**.
- Log in using your Gmail email address and password.

Gmail Interface Overview

Gmail's interface mirrors the convenience found in the Windows 11 Mail app, featuring a navigation pane on the left for folder access. It uniquely integrates Google Meet and Google Hangouts, enhancing the communication suite with video conferencing and messaging capabilities, respectively. The central area of the webpage is dedicated to displaying your emails, with unread messages and folders distinctly bolded for easy identification.

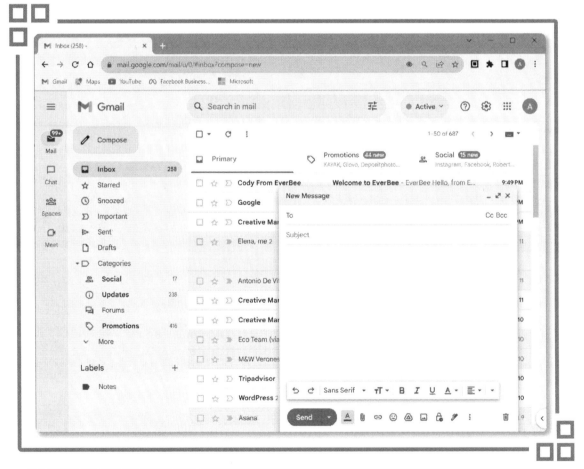

Managing Emails in Gmail

Sorting emails is streamlined with checkboxes for actions such as deleting, marking as read, or moving emails to different folders.

Composing Emails in Gmail

- Initiate a new email by clicking the **Compose** button, located in the upper left corner.

- A composition window appears in the bottom right, where you can add recipients, CC/BCC others, and specify a subject.

- The composition toolbar offers features like attaching files, inserting links or emojis, incorporating Google Drive files or photos, and toggling confidential mode.

- Additionally, schedule email delivery by clicking the arrow beside the **Send** button.

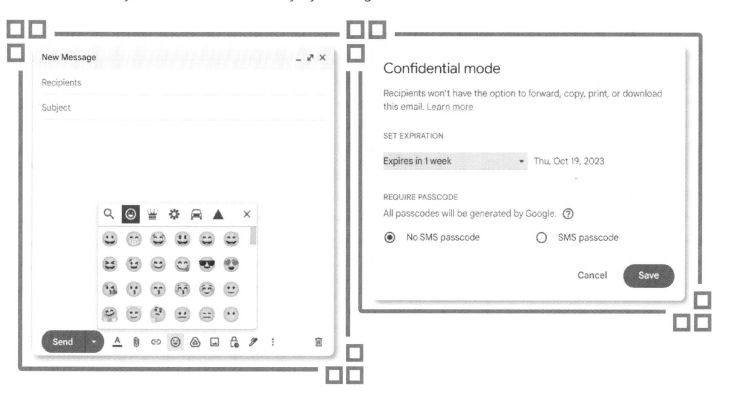

Customizing Gmail Preferences

Quick Settings Menu: Customize your Gmail appearance with options for layout, theme, inbox type, and reading pane.

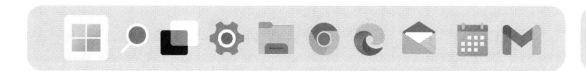

For comprehensive settings, click **"See all settings"**. This opens a new window with tabs for General, Labels, Inbox, Accounts and Import, Filters and Blocked Addresses, Forwarding and POP/IMAP, Add-ons, Chat and Meet, Advanced, Offline, and Themes.

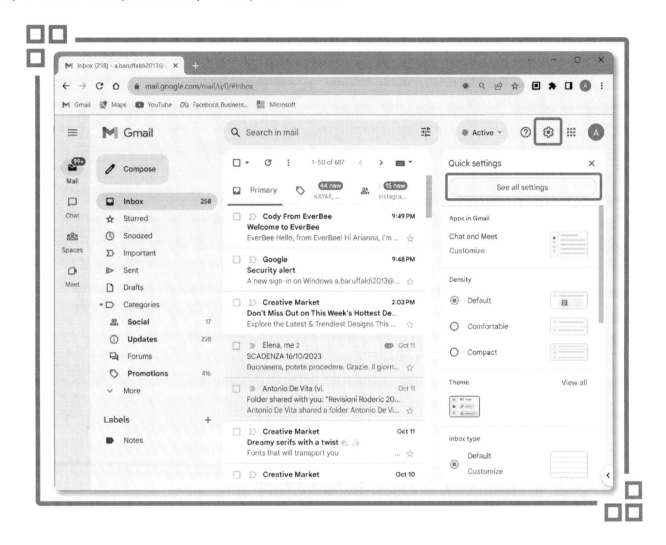

Chapter 10:

Leveraging Applications for Daily Efficiency in Windows 11

Windows 11 is equipped with a suite of applications designed to boost your productivity and streamline your daily routines. These applications are readily available through the Microsoft Store, enhancing your Windows experience with functionality and integration.

Microsoft Apps for Daily Use

Calendar

Embedded within Windows 11, the Calendar app provides a seamless way to organize your schedule. Access it quickly by clicking on the time and date on the right side of your taskbar, or launch it directly from the Start menu or taskbar.

Integration and Connectivity

The Calendar app works hand in hand with Mail, People, and To Do apps, allowing for an interconnected experience. Icons for these apps are located at the bottom of the navigation pane for easy access.

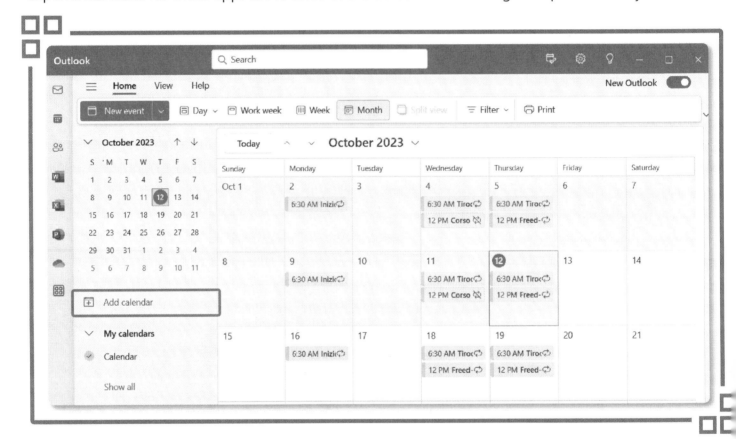

Adding an Account

To fully utilize the Calendar app, link it with an email account, such as Google or Microsoft.

- Navigate to **Settings > Manage accounts > Add account**, enter your credentials, and allow necessary permissions for synchronization.

- Multiple accounts can be added following these steps, consolidating your schedules across platforms.

Managing Calendars

The Calendar app supports the addition of various calendars, including personalized, birthdays, holidays, and contacts.

1) To add a new calendar, select **"Add calendars"** at the navigation pane's bottom and choose the desired type.

2) Calendars can be displayed or hidden by toggling the checkboxes next to each calendar's name, helping to declutter your view.

3) To remove a calendar, simply right-click it and choose **"Remove calendar."**

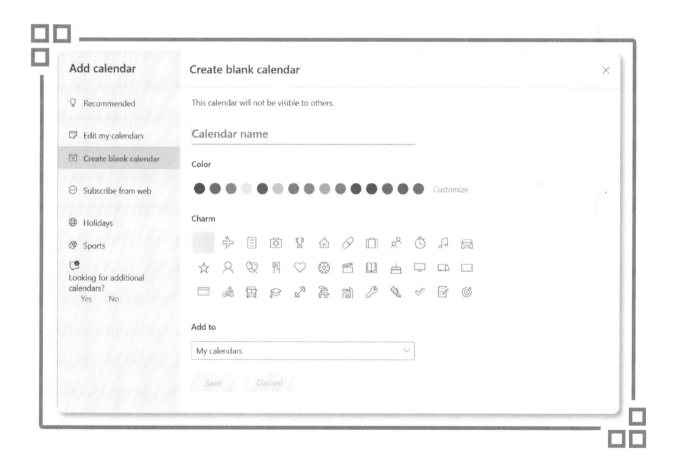

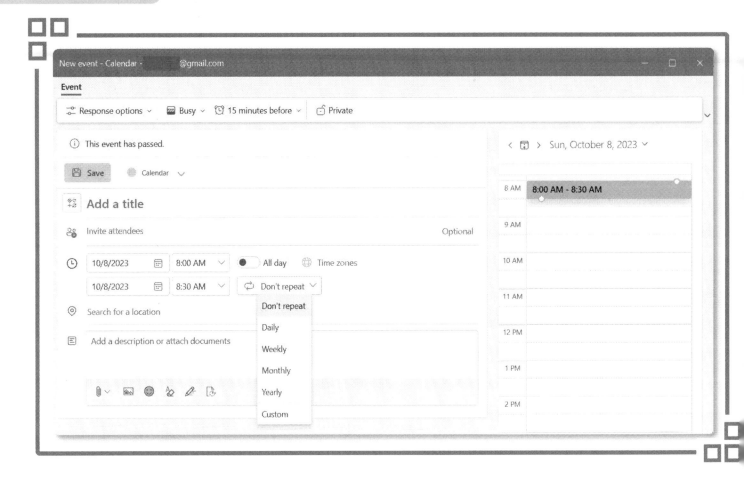

Creating Events in the Calendar App

Windows 11's Calendar app allows you to meticulously organize your schedule with various types of events. Here's how to make the most out of it:

Quick Event

1) **Start**: Launch the Calendar app and choose the day for your event.

2) **Details**: A pop-up window enables you to input the event's name, time, location, and reminders. By default, events are set to "All day".

3) **Customization**: You can select an icon or emoji for your event by clicking the circle next to the event name.

4) **Account Selection**: Change the associated account/calendar by selecting from the drop-down menu in the title bar.

5) **Save**: Confirm your event by clicking 'Save'.

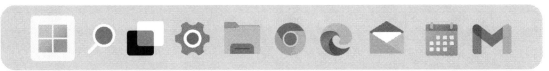

Detailed Event

1) **Access**: Opt for **"More details"** in the Quick Event pop-up or select **"New event"** from the top navigation pane.

2) **Fill In**: Enter comprehensive details such as the event name, calendar choice, and location. The app can suggest locations as you type.

3) **Notes**: Utilize the bottom text box to add any pertinent notes.

4) **Features**: The top toolbar offers options to save, delete, schedule meetings, set privacy, reminders, and recurrence.

5) **Invitations**: Use the right-hand contact list to invite participants.

6) **Finalize**: Hit 'Save' to add the event or 'Send' for group events with invitations.

Group Event

1) **Setup**: Create a group event by adding contacts to a detailed event. This event is then shared with invitees who will receive notifications.

2) **Invitations**: Click 'Send' to dispatch invites. Recipients can accept or decline your invitation.

Repeating Event

1) **Initiate**: From "New event", click "Repeat" on the toolbar to set up events that occur regularly.

2) **Frequency**: Decide on the repetition interval (daily, weekly, monthly, yearly) and customize further as needed.

3) **Duration**: Without an end date, the event repeats indefinitely.

4) **Confirmation**: Click 'Save' to schedule the recurring event in your calendar.

Sticky Notes:
Your Digital Post-it Notes on Windows 11

Sticky Notes in Windows 11 allows you to create digital notes reminiscent of physical post-it notes, perfect for quick reminders, motivational quotes, memories, or task lists.

Accessing Sticky Notes

Open the Sticky Notes app by searching for "sticky notes" in the Start menu. The app presents a straightforward interface with minimal buttons.

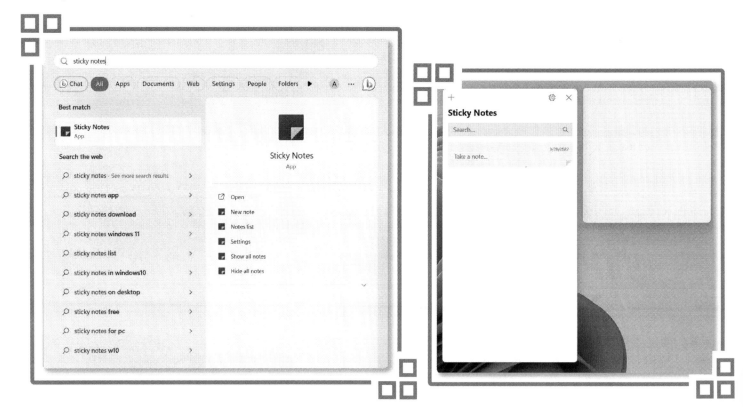

Customization Options

Toggle between light and dark modes through the settings menu, which also offers color adjustments, general settings, and sign-in options.

Signing into your Microsoft account is recommended to ensure your notes are saved securely.

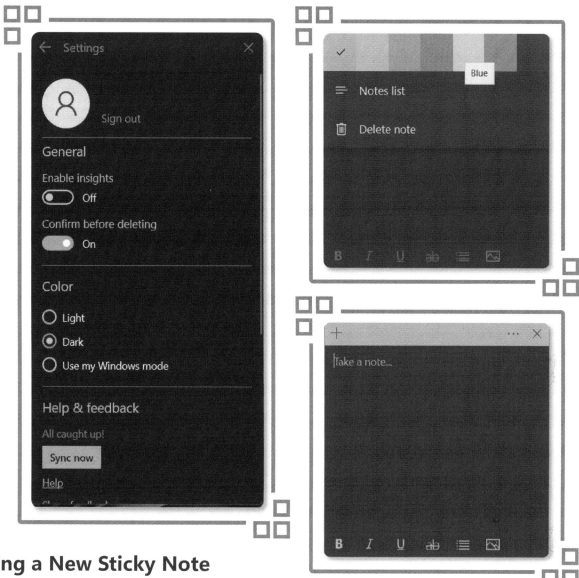

Creating a New Sticky Note

- **Initiate**: Click the + icon at the top right of the window to create a new sticky note, which will appear as a yellow note by default.

- **Edit and Format**: Type your note and utilize basic formatting tools to personalize it or add a picture.

- **Manage Notes**: The main window of the app will display a summary of your sticky notes.

- **Customize**: Change the note's color or delete it by clicking the Settings icon (three dots) on the note.

- **Persistence**: Your sticky notes remain accessible even after closing the app window.

- **Organization**: Differentiate and organize your sticky notes by employing various sizes and colors.

Bonus Chapter 11:

30 Quick Tips to Master Windows 11

Maximize your Windows 11 experience with these handy tips and tricks, designed to enhance productivity and user comfort.

1) **How to Take a Screenshot:**

   Press the **PrtScn** (or **Print Screen**) key to capture the entire screen. The image will be saved to the clipboard and can be pasted into a document or image editing program.

   To capture a specific window, press **Alt** + **PrtScn**. This will save only the active window to the clipboard.

2) **How to Immediately View the Desktop:**

   Press the **Windows** + **D** keys to minimize all open windows and show the desktop. Press again to restore the windows to their original state.

3) **How to Quickly Open Search:**

   Press the **Windows** + **S** keys to open the search bar, allowing you to search for files, settings, or apps on the PC.

4) **How to Quickly Lock Your PC:**

   Press the **Windows** + **L** keys to immediately lock the computer, useful when leaving your workstation and wanting to protect your privacy.

5) How to Open Task Manager:

Press **Ctrl** + **Shift** + **Esc** to open the Task Manager and check running applications or end processes that are not responding.

6) How to Change Virtual Desktops:

Press the **Windows** + **Tab** keys to open the task view, then click on "New desktop" at the top left to add a virtual desktop. Use **Ctrl** + **Windows** + **Right Arrow** or **Left Arrow** to switch between virtual desktops.

7) How to Zoom In/Out on the Desktop:

Hold down the **Ctrl** key and use the mouse wheel to zoom in or out on the desktop icons.

8) How to Quickly Open Settings:

Press the **Windows** + **I** keys to open the Settings app, where you can change system configuration, network options, user accounts, and more.

9) How to Start Voice Assistant Cortana:

Press the **Windows** + **C** keys to activate Cortana (if enabled in settings), allowing you to use voice commands to perform searches and commands.

10) How to Change Screen Brightness:

Open the Notification Center by clicking on the icon in the taskbar (or pressing **Windows** + **A**) and use the brightness slider to adjust the screen brightness.

11) Quick Access to Command Prompt or PowerShell:

Right-click on the Start button or press **Windows** + **X** and select "**Windows PowerShell**" or "**Command Prompt**" from the list.

12) Activate "Do Not Disturb" Mode:

Open the **Notification Center** (**Windows** + **A**) and click on "**Do Not Disturb**" to temporarily disable notifications.

13) Create Shortcuts on the Desktop:

Right-click on an empty area of the desktop, select "**New**" and then "**Shortcut**" to create a quick link to a file, folder, or application.

CHAPTER-11

14) Quickly Rename Files:

Select a file and press **F2** to rename it immediately without having to right-click.

15) Open File Explorer Quickly:

Press **Windows** + **E** to quickly open File Explorer.

16) Undo the Last Action:

Press **Ctrl** + **Z** to undo the last action performed, useful in many applications and in File Explorer.

17) Use the "Special Paste" Function in Office Applications:

After copying text or an image, use **Ctrl** + **Alt** + **V** to open the "Special Paste" menu in applications like Word or Excel, allowing you to choose the format of the pasted item.

18) Capture Specific Parts of the Screen:

Press **Windows** + **Shift** + **S** to launch the snipping tool that allows you to select and capture specific parts of the screen.

19) Restart File Explorer:

If File Explorer is not responding or you simply want to restart it, open Task Manager (**Ctrl** + **Shift** + **Esc**), find "File Explorer", right-click it and select "Restart".

20) Adjust the Size of Icons in File Explorer:

In File Explorer, press **Ctrl** and use the mouse wheel to increase or decrease the size of the icons.

21) Open Advanced System Settings:

Press **Windows** + **Pause** to quickly open the system properties and access advanced system settings.

22) Run Applications at Startup:

Type "Run" in the search bar and open the "Run" application. Type **shell:startup** to open the startup folder, where you can insert shortcuts to applications you want to automatically start when the PC turns on.

23) Quickly Empty the Recycle Bin:

Right-click on the Recycle Bin icon and select "Empty Recycle Bin" to permanently delete files.

24) Display File Extensions and Hidden Files:

In File Explorer, go to "View" in the top menu, then select "Options". In the window that opens, under the "View" tab, change the settings to display file extensions and hidden files.

25) Quickly Access Network Settings:

Press **Windows** + **I** and go to "Network & Internet" to quickly access network settings, Wi-Fi, and data usage.

26) Activate Night Light:

Open **Settings** (**Windows** + **I**), go to "System" and then "Display". Activate the "Night Light" to reduce eye strain in the evening hours, adjusting the screen colors to decrease the amount of blue light emitted.

27) Use Tablet Mode on Touchscreen Devices:

Open **Settings** (**Windows** + **I**), go to "System" and then "Tablet mode" to make Windows 11 more friendly on touchscreen devices, with larger icons and a simplified interface.

28) Customize the Taskbar:

Right-click on the taskbar, select "Taskbar settings" to customize the visibility of icons, the position of the taskbar, and other display options.

29) Use Virtual Desktops to Organize Work:

Press **Windows** + **Tab** to open the task view, then click on "New desktop" at the top left to create virtual desktops. You can move between virtual desktops with **Ctrl** + **Windows** + **Right Arrow** or **Left Arrow**, allowing you to organize applications and documents in separate workspaces.

30) Restore System Configuration:

In case of issues with Windows, you can restore the system to a previous point. Type "System Restore" in the search bar and follow the instructions to select a restore point at which the computer was functioning correctly.

Bonus Chapter 12:

Common FAQ for Navigating Windows 11

Discover quick solutions to frequently asked questions about Windows 11, helping you master the essentials of your operating system.

1) Finding and Accessing Files:

- Use the search icon in the taskbar or Windows key + S to start.
- Type the file or document's name.
- Click on the desired file from the search results. Tip: Organizing files in specific folders enhances search efficiency.

2) Enhancing Text and Icon Size:

- Accessibility is a priority in Windows 11.
- Navigate to **"Settings > System > Display"** to adjust the scale for better visibility.

3) Voice Typing Option:

- Windows 11 includes voice typing. Activate it with Windows + H and start speaking.
- Ideal for emails or documents, providing an alternative to keyboard typing.

4) Managing Multiple Windows:

- 'Snap Layouts' in Windows 11 allow for efficient window management.

- Hover over the maximize button of any window and choose a layout. This facilitates multitasking with multiple apps.

5) Recovering Deleted Files:

- No panic needed. Access the "Recycle Bin" from File Explorer.
- Find the deleted file, right-click, and choose "Restore" to revert it back to its original location.

6) Setting Reminders or Alarms:

- Utilize the "Alarms & Clock" app.
- Add new alarms or reminders in the 'Alarms' section by clicking the '+' symbol, keeping you on track with important tasks.

7) Windows 10-like Appearance:

- Yes, you can modify Windows 11 to resemble its predecessor.
- Right-click on the desktop, go to "Personalize," then "Start," and adjust the Start menu alignment to the left.

8) Avoiding Malicious Apps:

- For safety, use the Microsoft Store available on the taskbar.
- It provides a secure environment for app downloads, with all apps being vetted for security.

9) Addressing Mute PC Issues:

- If experiencing sound issues, check the speaker icon in the bottom-right.
- Make sure the volume is not muted. For persistent problems, troubleshoot sound issues directly from the speaker icon.

10) Video Chatting with Family:

- Windows 11 has Microsoft Teams built-in.
- Access Teams from the taskbar, sign in or set up an account, and use the video camera icon to start calls, keeping you connected with loved ones.

Conclusion

Windows 11 has been crafted with simplicity, intuitive organization, and an attractive interface to ensure even casual users can enhance their computing experience with some useful tips and tricks. Throughout this guide, we've explored the core elements that make working and playing on a Windows 11 device both confident and enjoyable.

We've witnessed the evolution of Windows, highlighting how recent features have broadened and transformed computer usage. Now, you should feel equipped to understand the hardware requirements for Windows 11, kickstart the upgrade process, and dive into the myriad of functionalities it offers.

Key Takeaways:

- **File Explorer Mastery**: You've learned to navigate, manage, and curate content efficiently, becoming adept at organizing and finding your files with ease.

- **Settings App Proficiency**: From managing your Microsoft account and signing options to customizing the taskbar and adjusting scaling options, you've gained the knowledge to tailor your OS to your liking.

- **Desktop Dynamics**: Mastering the Windows Desktop, you can now personalize your space with wallpaper, shortcuts, and even virtual desktops, making your computing environment uniquely yours.

- **Software Savvy**: Installing software through the Microsoft Store or your browser has become a breeze, ensuring you're equipped to enhance your PC's functionality while keeping it secure.

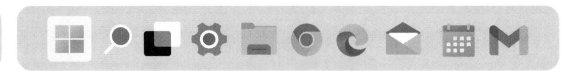

- **Web Browsing Wizardry**: With Google Chrome or Microsoft Edge, you're set to explore the world wide web, keeping tabs on the latest news, social media, and entertainment, and mastering bookmarks and tabs.

- **Email Enthusiasm**: The ability to craft and send engaging emails using the Windows 11 Mail app, including photos and GIFs, to stay connected with friends and family.

- **Teams for Connectivity**: Leveraging Microsoft Teams for video calls and meetings has never been easier, making remote communication efficient and enjoyable.

- **Productivity Power**: With access to to-do lists, calendars, and maps, you're ready to streamline your daily routines and navigate your tasks and travels with precision.

- **Photos App Creativity**: Organizing, editing, and sharing your memories through the Photos app brings your media library to life, allowing you to cherish and share moments with ease.

- **Gaming Glory**: Dive into the expansive world of gaming available on Windows 11, discovering a treasure trove of genres to explore and enjoy.

- **Tech Troubleshooting Triumphs**: Armed with shortcuts, hidden menus, and troubleshooting techniques, you're prepared to tackle challenges without reaching out for help.

This comprehensive overview of Windows 11 equips you with the knowledge to fully embrace and enhance your digital life, merging productivity with pleasure to make every day more efficient and enjoyable.

Glossary

It's easy to be perplexed by jargon and acronyms that seem foreign in today's tech-driven world. If you've ever been perplexed by terms like "RAM" or "web browser," you're not alone. Many seniors who did not grow up in the digital age may be perplexed by these terms. This is where this glossary comes in handy. We've compiled a list of common tech terms with simple explanations for the senior audience.

Antivirus: Software designed to detect, prevent, and remove malicious software such as viruses, worms, and trojans from your computer.

Application: Software that is installed on your computer and performs specific tasks or functions. They are also referred to as programs or software.

Backup: A secure copy of your data that is solely stored in a secure location to protect against data loss.

Bandwidth: The amount of data that can be transferred from and to your computer in a given amount of time.

Browser: An internet access and navigation application, such as Google Chrome, Microsoft Edge, or Firefox.

CPU: "Central processing unit," the unit that acts as the computer's "brain," performing arithmetic and logic calculations.

Crash: Occurs when a piece of software or hardware fails.

Cursor: The arrow on the screen that is connected to your mouse and is used to perform actions by clicking.

Default: The default settings or programs that come with your computer.

Desktop: Your computer's main directory or working area from which you access other directories and applications.

Disk: The storage device that is built into your computer.

Download: Mean download data from the internet, such as programs, photos, files and documents, or other media, into your computer.

Email: Is an abbreviation for "electronic mail," which is a digital message that can be sent via the internet.

Firewalls: are programs or pieces of hardware that are designed to prevent unauthorized access to a computer network or device.

Hardware: Hard drives, chips, keyboards, monitors, and other physical and mechanical components installed in your computer are examples of hardware.

Icons: are images that represent links to different programs or functions on your computer.

Input device: Any piece of hardware that you use to interact with your computer, such as a mouse, keyboard, microphone, and so on.

Install - Getting software or hardware ready for use.

Interface: Is a device, such as a monitor, or a program, such as a desktop, that allows you to communicate with your computer.

LAN (Local Area Network): is a network of interconnected computers in a specific geographic area, such as a home or office.

Memory: Information saved on your computer.

Menu: A list of options that can perform various functions. Pop-up menus, drop-down menus, and other options are possible.

Monitor: A screen or visual display that is linked to your computer.

Mouse: A piece of hardware that you move your hand around to control the on-screen cursor and click buttons.

MP3/MP4: Is a file format for storing video and audio data.

Network: Is a collection of interconnected computers.

Operating system: Software that manages all other software and hardware on your computer, laptop, or tablet, ensuring that all files, programs, and processes have efficient and adequate access to the hard drives, processing units, memory, and storage (Windows or MacOS are Operation System)

Plug and play: Hardware that can be plugged in and immediately recognized by the computer, allowing it to be used, such as a mouse, keyboard, hard drive, and so on.

Program: is synonymous with application.

RAM: 'Random access memory' is computer storage that is used to run background processes for various programs, allowing them to run faster.

Router: Is a device that connects multiple computer networks and routes data to its intended destination.

Software: Consists of computer programs and other data.

Virus: A piece of code that can replicate itself and cause damage to your computer or jeopardize its Zecurity. Malware is comparable.

Webcam: is a digital camera that is connected to your computer and can transmit live video to the internet.

Wi-Fi: is a wireless networking technology that enables computers and other devices to connect to the internet and wirelessly communicate with one another.

Window: is a section of your screen that displays the graphics of a program.

Word processor: Is a program that allows you to create, edit, and save documents.

GET YOUR FREE BOOK BONUSES NOW!

(DOWNLOAD FOR FREE WITH THE BELOW INSTRUCTION!)

Do you want to unlock the full potential of your Windows 11 Book?

1. 🎁 **COMPLETE CHAT-GPT BOOK:** *Unlock AI's full potential with our comprehensive Chat-GPT guide. Master every feature effortlessly!*

2. 🎁 **TIPS AND TRICKS TO PERSONALIZING WINDOWS 11:** *Transform your Windows 11 with simple, effective personalization tips. Make it truly yours!*

3. 🎁 **EXTRA-SAFE INTERNET BROWSING GUIDE:** *Browse safely with our essential guide. Protect your privacy and avoid online threats easily!*

SCAN THE QR CODE BELOW AND UNLOCK THE FULL POTENTIAL OF YOUR WINDOWS 11 GUIDE!

SCAN ME!

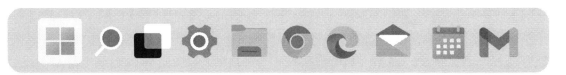

Index

123

Q INDEX